more than
COURAGEOUS

JOANNE SIMMONS

more than
COURAGEOUS

180
DEVOTIONS & PRAYERS
FOR A GIRL'S HEART

BARBOUR **kidz**

A Division of Barbour Publishing

Kristine, I'm beyond grateful for you and that God crossed our paths and gave us the gift of forever friendship—the loving, loyal kind like I wrote on page 65.

Published by Barbour Publishing, Inc., 1810 Barbour Drive, Uhrichsville, Ohio 44683, www.barbourbooks.com

Our mission is to inspire the world with the life-changing message of the Bible.

Member of the
Evangelical Christian
Publishers Association

Printed in the United States of America.

001130 0322 SP

Hey, courageous girl!

If you have asked Jesus to be your one and only Savior and have invited Him into your heart so that you can trust and follow Him forever, then you sure *are* courageous—and so much more! Do you know why? Because Jesus said so. Read it here from John 14:16–17 in the Bible: "I will ask My Father and He will give you another Helper. He will be with you forever. He is the Spirit of Truth. The world cannot receive Him. It does not see Him or know Him. You know Him because He lives with you and will be in you."

Wow! The one true almighty God is *in* you. So you are far more than just courageous—you are Spirit-filled. That Holy Spirit is God in Helper form, and you have Him at all times to lead you, to empower you, and to make you ready to face anything in life and do anything God your heavenly Father calls you to do. You are awesome because God within you is awesome. He created you, He loves you, and He has amazing plans for you. Just keep asking God to guide you, and let the following devotions help you learn and grow in His truth and love.

THE CREATOR CAN!

*I fall to my knees and pray to the Father, the Creator
of everything in heaven and on earth. I pray that from
his glorious, unlimited resources he will empower
you with inner strength through his Spirit.*
EPHESIANS 3:14–16 NLT

Think about all the powerful things in nature—the winds of a storm, strong rains of a downpour, mighty waves of the ocean, loud booms of thunder, flashing strikes of lightning. No human being can control those things. But the Creator of them sure can! And the same powerful Creator of all the world, who has everything under His control, is your loving heavenly Father. He is in you to help you through His Holy Spirit. With the almighty Creator on your side, you never have a thing to worry about or fear.

• •

**Dear God, You are the ultimate Creator. You are unlimited!
You can do anything! You are the most powerful of all! Please
help me to never forget these truths, and please fill me
up with Your inner strength through Your Spirit. Amen.**

YOU ARE A MASTERPIECE

For we are God's masterpiece. He has created us anew in Christ Jesus, so we can do the good things he planned for us long ago.
Ephesians 2:10 NLT

Have you ever made a masterpiece? Maybe an art project or invention that was especially cool. Maybe a creative musical number or story. Maybe new dance choreography or an athletic skill. Did you know that God, who created all of the amazing world and everything in it, considers people to be His masterpiece? And that includes you! Nothing else in all of creation is as wonderful and valuable as people because nothing else in all creation is created in God's image. And when God creates people, He makes us with good plans to do good things. You're even more than courageous, dear girl—you are a masterpiece, and your Master is in you through His Spirit to help you do all He designed you for.

• •

Dear God, thank You for being my good Master and for making me a masterpiece. I feel treasured when I think about how You love and value me, how You created me and designed the plans for my life. Show me those good plans and lead me in them every day. Amen.

THE SPIRIT HELPS YOU PRAY

The Holy Spirit helps us where we are weak. We do not know how to pray or what we should pray for, but the Holy Spirit prays to God for us with sounds that cannot be put into words. God knows the hearts of men. He knows what the Holy Spirit is thinking. The Holy Spirit prays for those who belong to Christ the way God wants Him to pray.
ROMANS 8:26–27

How do you feel when you pray? Do you sometimes feel silly or weak or overwhelmed and like you have no idea what to say? That's totally okay! God knows your heart and everything you think and say and do. And the Holy Spirit inside you knows how to tell God all about what you're going through and what you need.

• •

Dear God, I sure don't always know what to say to You or how to ask for help for myself and others. I'm so grateful that Your Holy Spirit is praying for me in perfect ways that I never could. Thank You for taking such good care of me! Amen.

FULL OF FRUIT

The fruit that comes from having the Holy Spirit in our lives is: love, joy, peace, not giving up, being kind, being good, having faith, being gentle, and being the boss over our own desires.
GALATIANS 5:22–23

With God's Holy Spirit inside, you should be full of fruit—no, not fruit salad fruit, but the kind of fruit the Bible talks about. These are the good things grown in you when you let the Holy Spirit work in and through your life. This fruit is "love, joy, peace, patience, kindness, goodness, faithfulness, gentleness, and self-control" (Galatians 5:22–23 NLT). What ways are you seeing this fruit grow in your life? Here's a fun idea: Draw a picture of a bowl of fruit. Then, inside each piece write down some of the ways your life is showing the fruit of the Spirit. Ask your family and friends to tell you how they are seeing good fruit in your life too!

• •

Dear God, please show me the ways the fruits of Your Spirit are growing well in me. I ask You to keep on growing these things in me—more and more and then even some more! Amen.

GOD WILL HOLD YOU UP

"Do not fear, for I am with you. Do not be afraid, for I am your God. I will give you strength, and for sure I will help you. Yes, I will hold you up with My right hand that is right and good. See, all those who are angry with you will be put to shame and troubled. Those who fight against you will be as nothing and will be lost. You will look for those who argue with you, but will not find them. Those who war against you will be as nothing, as nothing at all. For I am the Lord your God Who holds your right hand, and Who says to you, 'Do not be afraid. I will help you.' "

ISAIAH 41:10–13

God gave these words through His prophet Isaiah to the people of Israel. But these words are for you to remember today too so they will give you strength and courage. Is anyone mad at you or fighting against you? You'll be okay because God is with you, holding your hand, holding you up, helping you.

• •

Dear God, I don't want to be afraid of anyone or anything. You are my God who helps me and holds me up. Please don't let me ever forget that. Amen.

GOD'S GOOD NEWS

I am not ashamed of the Good News. It is the power of God. It is the way He saves men from the punishment of their sins if they put their trust in Him. It is for the Jew first and for all other people also. The Good News tells us we are made right with God by faith in Him. Then, by faith we live that new life through Him.

ROMANS 1:16–17

What's the best news you've heard lately? Everyone loves and needs good news, right? Well, the best good news is God's Good News. And when you believe and trust and share it—that God sent His Son, Jesus, to die to pay the price for sin and that Jesus rose to life again and will give all who believe in Him salvation and forever life too—then you are experiencing and sharing Good News. Don't keep that powerful Good News to yourself. Spread it around to everyone you can!

• •

Dear God, please help me to never be ashamed of Your awesome Good News about Jesus. Remind me that it has the power to save people from sin. Let Your Spirit in me help me to share it! Amen.

BEST BOOK EVER!

*[Jesus] said, "Yes, but those who hear the
Word of God and obey it are happy."*
LUKE 11:28

The Bible is anciently old, yet it applies to your life today. How is that possible? Because it is made alive by God. How cool is that? It helps you know how to live. It shows you what is wrong and how to be made right with God. It gives you everything you need to work well for God. And when you work well for God, you'll be a happy girl! God's Word says so! What a powerful book, the best book ever!

• •

Dear God, thank You for Your Word! Let it be alive and active in my life as I read it. Lead me in it and keep teaching me with it through Your powerful Holy Spirit. Amen.

GOOD GLIMPSES

The Holy Writings say, "No eye has ever seen or no ear has ever heard or no mind has ever thought of the wonderful things God has made ready for those who love Him." God has shown these things to us through His Holy Spirit. It is the Holy Spirit Who looks into all things, even the secrets of God, and shows them to us.

1 CORINTHIANS 2:9–10

What do you dream about the future? And what do you dream about heaven? As you dream, remember 1 Corinthians 1:9–10. We can never fully imagine how awesome the good things God has planned for us are! But if we stay strong in our faith in God, we can ask the Holy Spirit within us to show us good glimpses. What good glimpses are you seeing from God these days?

• •

Dear God, I trust You have amazing plans and blessings for my future—both here on earth and forever in heaven. Show me glimpses, please! Amen.

STAY IN THE LIGHT

God is light. There is no darkness in Him. If we say we are joined together with Him but live in darkness, we are telling a lie. We are not living the truth. If we live in the light as He is in the light, we share what we have in God with each other.

1 JOHN 1:5–7

Which sounds better to you? Living somewhere dark and dirty or light and clean? Sin makes us stay dirty in darkness, but confessing, meaning telling our sins to God, makes us clean and in the light again. No mistake or bad choice you make can ever cause God to love you less. He loves us always, no matter what. And He wants us to admit our sins to Him so He can wipe them away and help us live in the light and be a light to others.

• •

Dear God, I want to live in Your light and be clean from my sin. Help me to stay away from the darkness and dirtiness of sin. I confess these sins to You today:

_____

_____

Please forgive me. I know You love me and will take them away from me. Thank You! Amen.

HEADS-UP FROM THE HOLY SPIRIT

"And now I am bound by the Spirit to go to Jerusalem. I don't know what awaits me, except that the Holy Spirit tells me in city after city that jail and suffering lie ahead. But my life is worth nothing to me unless I use it for finishing the work assigned me by the Lord Jesus—the work of telling others the Good News about the wonderful grace of God."

ACTS 20:22–24 NLT

The Holy Spirit gave Paul a heads-up that bad things were going to happen to him, but Paul still felt led to go to Jerusalem. He knew he was supposed to do the work of telling others the Good News about Jesus saving people from their sins. Paul said his life was worth nothing unless he did this work. Paul can inspire us still today to know that even when the Holy Spirit gives us a heads-up that hard times are coming, we can still be faithful to the good works that God asks us to do, especially sharing His love and truth about Jesus.

Dear God, please warn me when trouble is coming, but don't let me be afraid of it or let it stop me from doing what You ask me to do. Amen.

GET A NEW MIND

Do not act like the sinful people of the world. Let God change your life. First of all, let Him give you a new mind. Then you will know what God wants you to do. And the things you do will be good and pleasing and perfect.

ROMANS 12:2

Sin is sadly so popular in our world. Which is why much of the time, it's good and wise to avoid what's popular. Sometimes doing so can make you feel left out and boring, but like the scripture says, let God give you a new mind about this. Let Him form in you a good attitude about feeling left out. When you're left out of what's popular, it often ends up protecting you from sin. In the times you feel left out, ask God for what He wants you to do with that time—the things that are good and pleasing and perfect to Him.

· ·

Dear God, help me not worry about being left out or being unpopular. Please help my mind think like Yours. Help me want what You want for me, and show me the good things You have planned for me, no matter what anyone else is doing. I trust You will provide for me all the right people and love and relationships I need in life. Amen.

GOD SEES YOU BEST, KNOWS YOU BEST, LOVES YOU BEST

O Lord, You have looked through me and have known me. You know when I sit down and when I get up. You understand my thoughts from far away. You look over my path and my lying down. You know all my ways very well. Even before I speak a word, O Lord, You know it all. You have closed me in from behind and in front. And You have laid Your hand upon me. All You know is too great for me. It is too much for me to understand. Where can I go from Your Spirit? Or where can I run away from where You are?

PSALM 139:1–7

You might think it's a family member or friend who knows you best, but no matter how close you are to your favorite people, no one sees and knows and loves you like God does. This chapter of scripture goes on to say, "You made all the delicate, inner parts of my body and knit me together in my mother's womb. Thank you for making me so wonderfully complex!" (Psalm 139:13–14 NLT).

• •

Dear God, thank You for knowing me so well (even the things I'm not proud of) and loving me no matter what. I'm so glad You see me and are with me anywhere I go. Amen.

BE THE GOOD GROUND PART I

"A man went out to plant seed. As he planted the seed, some fell by the side of the road. It was walked on and birds came and ate it. Some seed fell between rocks. As soon as it started to grow, it dried up because it had no water. Some seed fell among thorns. The thorns grew and did not give the seed room to grow. Some seed fell on good ground. It grew and gave one hundred times as much grain." When Jesus had finished saying this, He cried out, "You have ears, then listen!"

LUKE 8:5–8

Jesus loved to teach in parables or picture stories, like this one about seeds in the ground. We need to read His parables with minds and hearts that are ready and eager to listen and learn with the help of the Holy Spirit. What do you think this parable means?

• •

Dear God, help me to learn from the parables You taught. Help me know how these stories in the Bible apply to my life today and can help me grow closer to You. Amen.

BE THE GOOD GROUND PART 2

"This is what the picture-story means. The seed is the Word of God. Those by the side of the road hear the Word. Then the devil comes and takes the Word from their hearts. He does not want them to believe and be saved from the punishment of sin. Those which fell among rocks are those who when they hear the Word receive it with joy. These have no root. For awhile they believe, but when they are tempted they give up. Those which fell among thorns hear the Word but go their own way. The cares of this life let the thorns grow. A love for money lets the thorns grow also. And the fun of this life lets the thorns grow. Their grain never becomes full-grown. But those which fell on good ground have heard the Word. They keep it in a good and true heart and they keep on giving good grain."

LUKE 8:11–15

Jesus explained the parable, and His explanation helps us understand why some people seem to listen to God and His Word for a while but then later give up and go their own way. As you read and remember this parable, ask God for help from the Holy Spirit to constantly be the good ground that hears and keeps God's Word.

• •

Dear God, please help me to always be the good ground. Amen.

DO YOUR BEST

Where sin spread, God's loving-favor spread all the more. Sin had power that ended in death. Now, God's loving-favor has power to make men right with Himself. It gives life that lasts forever. Our Lord Jesus Christ did this for us. What does this mean? Are we to keep on sinning so that God will give us more of His loving-favor? No, not at all!

ROMANS 5:20–6:2

If Jesus saves people from sin, then why is it any big deal if people make bad choices and disobey God's Word? Because there are always bad consequences for sinful, bad choices. Anyone who says they love and follow Jesus but does not do their best to obey God's ways will certainly have a lot of trouble in life. That doesn't mean that doing your best to obey God's Word will lead to a perfect life with zero trouble. But it does mean God helps you through every trouble and works everything out for good for those who love Him (Romans 8:28).

• •

Dear God, I believe that all Your ways are the very best ways. Please help me to do my best to turn away from sin in all my choices. Amen.

PRAY FOR THOSE IN POWER

Pray for kings and all others who are in power over us so we might live quiet God-like lives in peace. It is good when you pray like this. It pleases God Who is the One Who saves. He wants all people to be saved from the punishment of sin. He wants them to come to know the truth. There is one God. There is one Man standing between God and men. That Man is Christ Jesus. He gave His life for all men so they could go free and not be held by the power of sin.

1 TIMOTHY 2:2–6

Sometimes you might not know exactly what to pray for, so come back to this scripture again and again. Pray for people in power of our nation and all other nations that they would let God's children live in peace and that Christians would be able to share the Good News of Jesus to help save people from their sin.

• •

Dear God, thank You that You want all people to know the truth about Jesus, that He gave His life to save them from sin. I pray for leaders here and all over the world to let Your Good News be shared freely—by me and all others who love You too. Amen.

GOD WINS EVERY BATTLE

Have joy and be happy with all your heart, O people of Jerusalem! The Lord has taken away your punishment. He has taken away those who hate you. The King of Israel, the Lord, is with you. You will not be afraid of trouble any more. On that day it will be said to Jerusalem: "Do not be afraid, O Zion. Do not let your hands lose their strength. The Lord your God is with you, a Powerful One Who wins the battle. He will have much joy over you. With His love He will give you new life. He will have joy over you with loud singing."

ZEPHANIAH 3:14–17

Let these words of the prophet Zephaniah encourage you today like they did the people of Jerusalem in ancient times. No matter what problem or trouble you're going through, no matter what enemy is working against you, God the Powerful One wins every battle for you in the end. Keep on trusting Him and letting Him strengthen you.

• •

Dear God, I trust that You win every battle. There is no one more powerful than You. Thank You for Your joy and victory in my life. Amen.

GOD KNOWS AND UNDERSTANDS

We have a great Religious Leader Who has made the way for man to go to God. He is Jesus, the Son of God, Who has gone to heaven to be with God. Let us keep our trust in Jesus Christ. Our Religious Leader understands how weak we are. Christ was tempted in every way we are tempted, but He did not sin. Let us go with complete trust to the throne of God. We will receive His loving-kindness and have His loving-favor to help us whenever we need it.

HEBREWS 4:14–16

How do you feel when someone truly listens and tries to understand you when you're upset? It's so helpful and comforting, right? We need people like that in our lives, and most importantly we need to remember that God truly listens to us and understands us best. Because Jesus became a human being just like us, He knows the kinds of temptations and weaknesses we have. Yet He did not sin but became sin for us (2 Corinthians 5:21) so that we could have a way to go to God and receive His love and His help and His salvation.

• •

Dear Jesus, thank You for understanding me and loving me and providing the way for God to listen to me and save me. Amen.

DON'T BE LAZY

Do not be lazy but always work hard. Work
for the Lord with a heart full of love for Him.
ROMANS 12:11

What makes you feel the laziest? Is it when you know you have a math worksheet you need to finish? Or when Mom says your room is a mess? Or Dad asks you to mow the lawn? Or you need to get ready for practice? We all have things we feel lazy about, but our lazy attitudes don't make those things go away. We're still going to have to do them. So when we think about every task as a job done for God with a "heart full of love for Him" like this scripture says, it can change our whole attitude and make our laziness go away. Try it and see what happens!

• •

Dear God, please help me not to be lazy. I don't have to love every task I need to do, but I should do each one with a heart of love for You. Help me to do my work with praise and gratitude to You in mind. Amen.

LIKE EAGLES

The God Who lives forever is the Lord, the One Who made the ends of the earth. He will not become weak or tired. His understanding is too great for us to begin to know. He gives strength to the weak. And He gives power to him who has little strength. Even very young men get tired and become weak and strong young men trip and fall. But they who wait upon the Lord will get new strength. They will rise up with wings like eagles. They will run and not get tired. They will walk and not become weak.

ISAIAH 40:28–31

When you feel weak and tired, remember that God gives strength and energy. If schoolwork or tough friendships or a stressful family life or health problems or anything at all is draining you, take time to focus on this scripture. Wait patiently on God to come to your rescue and make you rise up with wings like an eagle!

• •

Dear God, I am tired. I'm so glad that You never are. Please give me Your energy and strength to press on and overcome. Amen.

ALL KINDS OF SPECIAL WORK

The Lord said to Moses, "See, I have called by name Bezalel, the son of Uri, the son of Hur, of the family of Judah. I have filled him with the Spirit of God in wisdom, understanding, much learning, and all kinds of special work. He will plan good work in gold, silver and brass, in cutting stones to set, and in cutting wood, for all kinds of good work."

EXODUS 31:1–5

The Spirit of God filled a man named Bezalel with "wisdom, understanding, much learning, and all kinds of special work." God made him talented in working with gold, silver, brass, stone, and wood. What areas do you have talent in? Do you recognize those talents are from God and thank Him for the ways He has filled you with His Spirit to do certain things especially well? Give God all the glory and praise and keep asking Him every day to show you how He wants you to use the special abilities He has given you.

• •

Dear God, thank You for filling me with Your Spirit to do special things and have unique talents. I never want to take these gifts for granted. They are all from You and all for You! Amen.

GET RID AND KEEP RUNNING

Let us put every thing out of our lives that keeps us from doing what we should. Let us keep running in the race that God has planned for us. Let us keep looking to Jesus. Our faith comes from Him and He is the One Who makes it perfect.

HEBREWS 12:1–2

What do you think are the things in your life that keep you from doing what you should, like this scripture talks about? Do you spend too much time doing silly things that don't matter instead of good things that God has planned for you? We all do at times, and we all need to constantly look at our lives to see where we need to get rid of things that aren't good for us and keep us away from God's will. Thankfully, the Holy Spirit in us is happy to help!

• •

Dear God, please help me see what I need to put out of my life that keeps me from doing the good things You want me to do. Help me to run the race You have planned for me in the very best way I can! Amen.

SHINE BRIGHT

"You are the light of the world. You cannot hide a city that is on a mountain. Men do not light a lamp and put it under a basket. They put it on a table so it gives light to all in the house. Let your light shine in front of men. Then they will see the good things you do and will honor your Father Who is in heaven."

MATTHEW 5:14–16

You are the light of the world because the Holy Spirit is in you! Every good thing you do helps point others to knowing Jesus as Savior and having the Holy Spirit and honoring God the Father in heaven. So don't ever hide your light. Let it shine so bright for everyone to see!

• •

Dear God, please remind me every day that I am shining Your light through Your Holy Spirit within me, and I am meant to shine brightly! Please let others see Your light in me and want to know and honor You. Amen.

LET THE BIRDS REMIND YOU

"Not one of the birds falls to the earth without your Father knowing it. God knows how many hairs you have on your head. So do not be afraid. You are more important than many small birds."

MATTHEW 10:29–31

Every time you hear a bird chirp or tweet or sing its song, think of this scripture and let it remind you that God knows every single bird that lives on the earth at this very moment. He knows exactly where it is and what it does. And He also knows you so well that He even has counted the hairs on your head. No one else does that! That shows you how much God cares about you and loves you and protects you. You are so important to Him that He literally let His Son die to take away your sin and save you. Don't ever forget that truth, dear girl, and let every bird remind you of it.

Dear God, I can't even begin to understand how You know everything about everything and everything about me too. But I am so grateful for Your love and care. I'm so grateful You gave Jesus to save me from my sin. Amen.

JOY INSTEAD OF FEAR

I will honor the Lord at all times. His praise will always be in my mouth. My soul will be proud to tell about the Lord. Let those who suffer hear it and be filled with joy. Give great honor to the Lord with me. Let us praise His name together. I looked for the Lord, and He answered me. And He took away all my fears. They looked to Him and their faces shined with joy.

PSALM 34:1–5

Think about what scares you, the fears that are in your life right now. Do the fears go away if you focus on them? How could they? They grow bigger in your mind if you let them have lots of room in there. So don't! Instead, give God lots of room in your amazing brain. Look for Him, meaning focus on Him, through reading His Word, singing praise to Him, and praying to Him. Ask Him to show Himself to you in all kinds of ways. Then just see how He takes away all your fears and how He makes your face shine with joy!

Dear God, please help me to take my focus off my fears and put my focus on You instead. Fill my mind and heart with thoughts of You and praise to You! Make my face shine with joy, no matter what. Amen.

YOUR HELPER WILL REMIND YOU

The Helper is the Holy Spirit. The Father will send Him in My place. He will teach you everything and help you remember everything I have told you.

JOHN 14:26

Do you ever need help remembering the things you've been taught—at school, at home, at church, and everywhere you learn something new? Of course you do! We all do. When Jesus was on earth, He was so kind to let His followers know that when He left the earth God the Father would not leave them alone to try to remember everything Jesus taught. God would send the Helper, His Holy Spirit, in place of Jesus, to teach and remind them. And the very same Holy Spirit is in you and helping you today because you trust in Jesus as your Savior.

• •

Dear God, You know people so well—You know that we all need Your help to remember all of Jesus' teachings. I am so grateful for my constant Helper, Your Holy Spirit. Thank You for being with me, for guiding me, for teaching me, and for reminding me every moment of every day. Amen.

ALWAYS STRONGER

*The One Who lives in you is stronger
than the one who is in the world.*

1 JOHN 4:4

The world can feel upside-down crazy sometimes, right? How are you noticing that in your life? We have an enemy, the devil, who loves to spread sin and evil as much as he can (1 Peter 5:8; 1 John 5:19). Even when things do seem out of control in the world around you, you always have hope and power and strength because of God's Holy Spirit living in you. Memorize 1 John 4:4, and then put it on repeat in your beautiful brain. God is always stronger than the devil. God never leaves you and will help you fight and win against any evil plan any enemy has against you.

• •

**Dear God, don't let me forget that You are always
stronger within me than the evil one who is in the
world. Give me strength and boldness and courage
and confidence as I remember the power of Your
Word and Your Holy Spirit within me. Amen.**

LET GOD TAKE CARE OF IT PART 1

When someone does something bad to you, do not pay him back with something bad. Try to do what all men know is right and good. As much as you can, live in peace with all men. Christian brothers, never pay back someone for the bad he has done to you. Let the anger of God take care of the other person. The Holy Writings say, "I will pay back to them what they should get, says the Lord." "If the one who hates you is hungry, feed him. If he is thirsty, give him water. If you do that, you will be making him more ashamed of himself." Do not let sin have power over you. Let good have power over sin!

ROMANS 12:17–21

Ugh, this is a tough one to obey sometimes, right? When someone does something mean to you, usually your first reaction is to do something mean right back—even if just in your mind. God says don't do that. Let Him take care of making things right. Instead, you should act loving and kind, letting "good have power over sin."

• •

Dear God, please help me to obey You in this way—to not want to give payback when someone treats me badly. I trust that You will make things right. Please help me to let good have power over sin. Amen.

LET GOD TAKE CARE OF IT PART 2

Love each other with a kind heart and with a mind that has no pride. When someone does something bad to you, do not do the same thing to him. When someone talks about you, do not talk about him. Instead, pray that good will come to him. You were called to do this so you might receive good things from God.

1 PETER 3:8–9

Instead of paybacks, pray for good things to come to the person who did you wrong. What? That seems so upside down, right? But it's what God has called you to do, and when you obey Him in this, He will bless you and give you good things.

• •

Dear God, help my heart to be truly kind and my mind to have no pride. Help me to obey You in wanting good things for those who do bad to me. You know and see all things, and You will bless me for doing Your will. Amen.

LISTEN TO FELLOW FOLLOWERS

We looked for the Christians and stayed with them seven days. The Christians had been told by the Holy Spirit to tell Paul not to go to Jerusalem. When our time was up, we left there and went on our way. All of them with their wives and children went with us out of town. They got down on their knees on the shore and prayed. After we said good-bye, we got on the ship and they went back to their houses.

ACTS 21:4–6

You might read this and wonder why the Holy Spirit didn't just tell Paul directly that he should not go to Jerusalem. We don't know for sure. But we should realize that many times we must listen to other Christians to help us know what to do. God can use any way He wants to speak to us and guide us, and He often uses our fellow followers of Jesus. It's so important to have good, close friends in our lives who also trust in Jesus as Lord and Savior.

Dear Jesus, please help me to always have good friends in my life who know and love and follow You like I do. Let the Holy Spirit lead them as the Holy Spirit leads me too. Let us help one another and encourage one another. Amen.

HE RIDES ON THE WINGS OF THE WIND

Praise the Lord, O my soul! O Lord my God, You are very great. You are dressed with great honor and wonderful power. He covers Himself with light as with a coat. He spreads out the heavens like a tent. He makes His home on the waters. He makes the clouds His wagon. He rides on the wings of the wind.

PSALM 104:1–3

Is something overwhelming you today? Maybe family or friend trouble or trouble at school? Maybe you feel weak and powerless to do anything to fix the trouble. Maybe you feel like you need a superhero from the movies to come flying in to rescue you. If that's the case, let Psalm 104 remind you of the One who lives within you. The Spirit of God who "rides on the wings of the wind" does! He truly is your superhero who never leaves you on your own. Talk to Him, ask for His help with everything, pray to Him, and praise Him.

• •

Dear God, remind me every day that You ride on the wings of the wind. You are my superhero! Please help me when I am overwhelmed. Please help me with everything. Amen.

NUTS AND BANANAS

*Most of all, have a true love for each
other. Love covers many sins.*
1 PETER 4:8

Have you had any fits or fights with your siblings or your mom or dad or someone in your home lately? It's sure hard not to! Sometimes it feels like family—the ones you're supposed to love the most and be loved by the most—are the ones you struggle with the worst. But remember that it makes sense that the more time you are together in your home, the more opportunities there are to drive one another totally nuts and bananas. Focus on this scripture and pray it for your family—that you all would have true love, God's kind of love, for one another. Then let that love cover the sins that happen when you're not getting along. Through His Holy Spirit in you, ask for God's help and forgiveness in your family life.

• •

Dear God, even when we're going totally nuts and bananas, please help my family and me to have true love for one another. We only know how to love at all because You first loved us. Please cover our sins with love that comes from You. Amen.

WHAT ARE YOU THINKING ABOUT?

Keep your minds thinking about whatever is true, whatever is respected, whatever is right, whatever is pure, whatever can be loved, and whatever is well thought of. If there is anything good and worth giving thanks for, think about these things.

PHILIPPIANS 4:8

What do you watch, read, and listen to on TV and the internet, in books, and through music? It all matters. It all affects who you are. The world will try to tell you even the bad stuff is all just for fun, but don't listen to the world; listen to God, especially through His Word. In the book of Philippians, the apostle Paul said to keep our minds thinking about what is true, respected, right, pure, lovable, good, and worthy of our thanks. Whenever you put a thought or idea into your mind, ask yourself if it matches up to this scripture.

• •

Dear God, help me to always be thinking about good things. Help me to be careful about what I allow into my mind through TV, internet, books, social media, music, and everything else. Amen.

LET JESUS HELP YOU

"Come to Me, all of you who work and have heavy loads. I will give you rest. Follow My teachings and learn from Me. I am gentle and do not have pride. You will have rest for your souls. For My way of carrying a load is easy and My load is not heavy."
MATTHEW 11:28–30

When something feels heavy or troubling in your life, Jesus wants to help you with it. Another scripture says, "Give all your worries to Him because He cares for you" (1 Peter 5:7). When you're tired and struggling, isn't it nice when someone comes along and says, "Come here. Let me help you with that"? That's what Jesus was saying. Talk to Him about every problem you have. Confess your sins to Him. Follow the ways of Jesus and learn from Him, and you will have the rest and care you need.

• •

Dear Jesus, thank You for letting me come to You with all my heavy and hard things. Thank You for helping and giving me rest and peace. I always want to learn from You and live for You. Amen.

HONORING MOM AND DAD

"Honor your father and your mother, so your life may be long in the land the Lord your God gives you."
EXODUS 20:12

You might feel like you need extra, extra, *extra* help from God's Holy Spirit to respectfully obey your parents. It's hard sometimes, for sure. But if it's important to God, it should be important to you. In the Ten Commandments, God said to honor Dad and Mom so that you'll be blessed. Remember that the next time you feel like refusing to help with chores or go to bed on time. God isn't trying to ruin all your fun. He wants to reward you for obeying His Word by honoring your parents. Let Him teach and guide and help you to do this.

• •

Dear God, I sure don't always feel like honoring Mom and Dad. I want to do my own thing—that's way more fun! But please help me remember what You want me to do. I love You, and I love my parents. Help me to honor them the way I should. Amen.

BE SURE OF GOD

The Lord is my light and the One Who saves me. Whom should I fear? The Lord is the strength of my life. Of whom should I be afraid? When sinful men, and all who hated me, came against me to destroy my flesh, they tripped and fell. Even if an army gathers against me, my heart will not be afraid. Even if war rises against me, I will be sure of You.

PSALM 27:1–3

Wow, what courage and confidence this psalm can give you! With the Lord as your Light and the One who saves you, nothing and no one should ever make you feel afraid. You can always be absolutely sure of Him—sure of His strength and power and protection and especially sure of His great love for you.

• •

Dear God, thank You that I can be absolutely sure of Your strength! Amen.

RIGHT AT HOME

Do you not know that your body is a house of God where the Holy Spirit lives? God gave you His Holy Spirit. Now you belong to God. You do not belong to yourselves. God bought you with a great price. So honor God with your body. You belong to Him.

1 CORINTHIANS 6:19–20

It seems a little funny to think of your body as a house, but the Bible says it is! And God loves to make Himself at home in you. He lives right within you through His Holy Spirit. He never, ever leaves you, and He wants you to honor Him in all that you do. You belong to Him, and that's such a blessing because He wants to take the best care of you and lead you in the life He has planned for you.

• •

Dear God, You are welcome to make Yourself right at home in me. I'm grateful You never leave me. Please help me to honor You in all that I do. Please show me how. Amen.

OBEY THE WORD OF GOD

*Obey the Word of God. If you hear only and
do not act, you are only fooling yourself.*

JAMES 1:22

Pretend Mom or Dad or a teacher at school gives you a list of things to do. You listen to the list or you read it and think, *This is a nice list. There are some good, important things on this list.* And then you put it down and go on your way without doing the things you were supposed to. How will that go for you? Probably not good; probably you'll be facing some bad consequences. We're supposed to obey parents and obey teachers when they give us tasks we need to do. You can think of the Bible in a similar way (though it's so much more than just a to-do list!). If you don't obey it, you are being foolish! There will be bad consequences for you. God gave us the Bible as a guide for life, and when we follow it, we live good lives. When we don't follow it, we're just asking for trouble.

**Dear God, please help me to not only hear
and read Your Word but obey it and actually
do what it says. Show me and lead me. Amen.**

BE FILLED WITH WONDER PART I

In the beginning God made from nothing the heavens and the earth. The earth was an empty waste and darkness was over the deep waters. And the Spirit of God was moving over the top of the waters. Then God said, "Let there be light," and there was light.

GENESIS 1:1–3

You probably know that you can find the true story of God creating the world and everything in it in Genesis, the first book of the Bible. But when was the last time you read the creation account for yourself? Go read it carefully now. As you read, ask God to fill you with total wonder at how awesome He is. Think about how He was able to just say the words and form the earth and fill it and create anything He wanted. He still can today too. Remember that the powerful, creative Spirit of God in Genesis 1 is the same Holy Spirit living within you and loving you right now. Amazing!

• •

Dear God, fill me with wonder again and again about how incredible You are, how incredible it is that You live within me. Amen.

BE FILLED WITH WONDER PART 2

"Ask the wild animals, and they will teach you. Ask the birds of the heavens, and let them tell you. Or speak to the earth, and let it teach you. Let the fish of the sea make it known to you. Who among all these does not know that the hand of the Lord has done this? In His hand is the life of every living thing and the breath of all men."

JOB 12:7–10

Be filled with wonder as you read God's Word and be filled with more wonder as you experience God's creation every day. Did you hear a bird chirp today? Did you see a flower or even just a single blade of grass? Did you feel a breeze or a raindrop or some sunshine on your face? All of it—the mighty things of creation and the sweet, simple things too—came to be from our awesome Creator God. He created everything, He created you, He lives in you, He loves you.

· ·

Dear God, through Your Word, through Your creation, and through anything You want, please show me more and more of who You are and how much You love me. You are truly wonderful, and I praise You! Amen.

WALKING ON WATER PART 1

Just before the light of day, Jesus went to them walking on the water. When the followers saw Him walking on the water, they were afraid. They said, "It is a spirit." They cried out with fear. At once Jesus spoke to them and said, "Take hope. It is I. Do not be afraid!" Peter said to Jesus, "If it is You, Lord, tell me to come to You on the water." Jesus said, "Come!"

MATTHEW 14:25–29

Put yourself in the disciples' sandals in this scene. Would you have been afraid at first like them, or do you think you would have recognized Jesus right away? And then would you have been bold like Peter, ready to walk on water too? Why or why not?

• •

Dear Jesus, help me to be bold like Peter. I trust You to help me do things that are courageous! Amen.

WALKING ON WATER PART 2

Peter got out of the boat and walked on the water to Jesus. But when he saw the strong wind, he was afraid. He began to go down in the water. He cried out, "Lord, save me!" At once Jesus put out His hand and took hold of him. Jesus said to Peter, "You have so little faith! Why did you doubt?" When Jesus and Peter got into the boat, the wind stopped blowing. Those in the boat worshiped Jesus. They said, "For sure, You are the Son of God!"

MATTHEW 14:29–33

Again, put yourself in this true story. Would you have started to focus on the wind and be afraid, or would you have kept your eyes on Jesus? Whatever your answer, let this story remind you to not take your eyes off Jesus in any situation. Through the Holy Spirit, Jesus is always with you to help you with His great and supernatural power, so we have no reason to be afraid.

• •

Dear Jesus, help me to never doubt You. I believe You are truly the Son of God, You are my Savior, and You are always with me through the Holy Spirit. Amen.

WONDERFULLY UNIQUE

There are different kinds of gifts. But it is the same Holy Spirit Who gives them. There are different kinds of work to be done for Him. But the work is for the same Lord. There are different ways of doing His work. But it is the same God who uses all these ways in all people. The Holy Spirit works in each person in one way or another for the good of all.

1 CORINTHIANS 12:4–7

Think about what connects you to your best friends. It's so fun to find people we have a lot in common with. But no two people are exactly the same, and there sure are lots of differences among friends too. That's a good thing! God made us each unique when He created us, and the Holy Spirit gives us all different gifts and abilities. We can use them all to do good in the world and help one another—and most of all to give praise to God our Creator and point others to knowing our Savior Jesus Christ.

· ·

Dear God, show me my special gifts and abilities, and keep me working hard for You. I want to love and serve others in the ways You designed me for. Amen.

YOU NEED GOD'S WISDOM

*If you do not have wisdom, ask God for it. He is always
ready to give it to you and will never say you are wrong
for asking. You must have faith as you ask Him. You
must not doubt. Anyone who doubts is like a wave
which is pushed around by the sea. Such a man will
get nothing from the Lord. The man who has two
ways of thinking changes in everything he does.*
JAMES 1:5–8

To be even more than courageous, you need God's wisdom *all.
the. time.* Thankfully God never, ever leaves you, and He loves to
give you wisdom. You can never bother Him by asking for more
and more and *more.* As you ask, be sure you believe that He gives
it and then ask Him for His help to apply that wisdom in every
area of your life.

• •

**Dear God, thank You that You love to give me wisdom.
Please help me not to forget to ask for it all the time.
Then help me not to doubt You. I trust that You give me
wisdom, and I trust that You will help me to use it. Amen.**

BECAUSE THEY HAD FAITH

Because Sarah had faith, she was able to have a child long after she was past the age to have children. She had faith to believe that God would do what He promised. Abraham was too old to have children. But from this one man came a family with as many in it as the stars in the sky and as many as the sand by the sea. These people all died having faith in God. They did not receive what God had promised to them. But they could see far ahead to all the things God promised and they were glad for them.

HEBREWS 11:11–13

If you're ever feeling not good enough, not strong enough, not courageous enough, or simply not enough, go to Hebrews 11 to see examples of Bible heroes who did amazing things, not because of who they were or how good they were or how strong they were or how courageous they were but because they had great faith in God. Let their examples help you believe in God's power and might and ability to do absolutely anything in and through you!

• •

Dear God, please grow my faith to be so big and then even bigger. Through Your Spirit working in me, please use me for Your will and Your glory. Amen.

FOCUS ON OTHERS

Keep having the same love. Be as one in thoughts and actions. Nothing should be done because of pride or thinking about yourself. Think of other people as more important than yourself. Do not always be thinking about your own plans only. Be happy to know what other people are doing.

PHILIPPIANS 2:2–4

Selfishness comes naturally and easily to us. Is your first thought to give the best piece of pizza in the box or the best brownie in the pan to someone else or to yourself? We have to work kinda hard sometimes to actually think and care about others more than ourselves. It's good God loves to help us with this! Ask the Holy Spirit within you to help you focus first on others, not yourself. That never means you are worthless or don't need good care too, but let God love and care for you through others, just as He loves and cares for others through you.

• •

Dear God, please help me not to be focused on myself but more focused on others and how You want me to share Your love with them. I know You are always loving and taking care of me through others too. Amen.

THE ONE WHO MADE ALL LIGHT

*Whatever is good and perfect comes to us from God.
He is the One Who made all light. He does not change.
No shadow is made by His turning. He gave us our new
lives through the truth of His Word only because He
wanted to. We are the first children in His family.*

JAMES 1:17–18

God is the One who made all light. Think of that when things feel dark and shadowy and sad around you. Ask God to show you more and more of His good and perfect light and to help you remember that every good and perfect gift and blessing in your life comes from Him. Notice both the simplest things, like a cool breeze on a hot day, and the biggest things, like a major dream come true. Nothing in the world can change the fact that God your Father has given you a bright new life through Jesus Christ.

• •

**Dear God, You are my good Father and I am Your child.
Thank You for that promise that never, ever changes. Show
me more and more how you are the One who made all light,
the One who gives every gift and blessing in my life. Amen.**

HOW TO BEST TAKE A TEST

*My Christian brothers, you should be happy when you
have all kinds of tests. You know these prove your faith.
It helps you not to give up. Learn well how to wait so you
will be strong and complete and in need of nothing.*

JAMES 1:2–4

To be even more than courageous, you need to know how to best take a test. No, not just the ones at school but the ones that come to you through the hard things in life, the ones that prove whether your faith is real—whether you really trust in God or not. When you're going through a bad time, how should you respond? Should you throw a fit? Should you just quit? Or should you keep on trusting that God is in you through His Holy Spirit and will help you and provide for you, even if you have to wait a while for Him to come to the rescue?

• •

**Dear God, help me to take tests well. Help me to be
happy that they prove my faith in You when I don't
give up in the middle of them. Help me to never stop
trusting You, even when I have to wait on You. Amen.**

COURAGE AND CONFIDENCE

For You made the parts inside me. You put me together inside my mother. I will give thanks to You, for the greatness of the way I was made brings fear. Your works are great and my soul knows it very well. My bones were not hidden from You when I was made in secret and put together with care in the deep part of the earth. Your eyes saw me before I was put together. And all the days of my life were written in Your book before any of them came to be.

PSALM 139:13–16

No one knows you better than the one true God who made you. And He loves you and never leaves you. He planned all the days of your life before you were even born. That can give you so much courage and, even more, such confidence. The God of all the universe put every piece of you together, and He loves you most and wants what's best for you in all things. Since that is true, don't ever let anyone put you down!

Dear God, please help me not to forget that You designed me and the plans for my life. Let all my courage and confidence come from You! Amen.

IN EACH STEP

Let the Holy Spirit lead you in each step. Then you will not please your sinful old selves. The things our old selves want to do are against what the Holy Spirit wants. The Holy Spirit does not agree with what our sinful old selves want.

GALATIANS 5:16–17

Think of times when you've needed to be led in each step. Maybe when you were learning new choreography? Or when you were on a really tough hike in the woods or mountains? Every day, you need to be led in each step to live a life that is pleasing to God. All on your own, you will do what your old sinful self wants. But with God's Holy Spirit in you, you can let Him lead you to do what He wants for you. And since He made you and loves you more than anyone else, you can trust that what He wants is always best!

• •

Dear God, I want You to lead me in each step of my life. When I start to go my own way, please guide me back to You. I know what You want is always what's best. Amen.

YOUR SAFE AND STRONG PLACE

O Lord, in You I have found a safe place. Let me never be ashamed. Set me free, because You do what is right and good. Turn Your ear to me, and be quick to save me. Be my rock of strength, a strong place to keep me safe. For You are my rock and my safe place.

PSALM 31:1–3

Focus on all the ways God is described in this scripture. He is your safe place. He does what is right and good. He is your Rock of strength. He is your strong place. And remember, He never, ever leaves you, because His Holy Spirit is within you! When you're going through a tough or scary time, how can focusing on this scripture make you courageous and so much more? Think about ways God has already helped you through hard things in the past, and trust that He will always do so in the future because He is your safe and strong place.

• •

Dear God, thank You for being safe and strong. Thank You for always doing what is right and good. Thank You for never leaving me. I trust You and love You. Amen.

GOD WILL FREE YOU

*For the honor of Your name, lead me and show me the
way. You will free me from the net that they have hidden
for me. For You are my strength. I give my spirit into Your
hands. You have made me free, O Lord, God of truth.*

PSALM 31:3–5

Have you ever felt like someone has a net hidden and ready to trap
you, like this scripture talks about? Maybe someone you thought
was a friend isn't really feeling like a friend anymore. Maybe they
seem to want to embarrass or hurt you or get you in trouble. Ask
God to lead and show you the way out of that situation. Ask God
to show you the truth and give you wisdom. Ask God to help you
talk about the problem with trusted grown-ups who will help too.

• •

**Dear God, please lead and show me the way out of any
trap in my life. Help me to know the truth. Help me to
remember that I am so loved and I am free in You. Amen.**

LET GOD DO SOMETHING NEW

"Do not remember the things that have happened before. Do not think about the things of the past. See, I will do a new thing."

ISAIAH 43:18–19

In this scripture, God was telling His people, the Israelites, to forget the hard times of the past and let Him bring them into something new and good. Do you have hard times you need to forget too? Maybe you feel like last school year was just awful, and it makes you worried about the new school year coming up. But be glad last year is done and let it go! Let God help you every moment of every day. Let His wonderful grace cover you and His amazing love fill you up. Let Him protect you and lead you. Let Him do the new things He wants to do in you and through you.

• •

Dear God, help me to forget what I need to forget and focus on the awesome new things You are doing. You are in me, and my life is from You and for You. Cover me with Your amazing grace. Fill me with Your love. Amen.

HARDWORKING AND HAPPY PART 1

God is helping you obey Him. God is doing what He wants done in you. Be glad you can do the things you should be doing. Do all things without arguing and talking about how you wish you did not have to do them. In that way, you can prove yourselves to be without blame. You are God's children and no one can talk against you, even in a sin-loving and sin-sick world. You are to shine as lights among the sinful people of this world.
PHILIPPIANS 2:13–15

Think about your least favorite chores and homework assignments. What is your attitude like when you do them? How can remembering this scripture in Philippians 2 help you adjust your attitude? It does seem impossible sometimes to do the jobs and assignments you hate without grumbling or complaining, but never forget that "God is helping you obey Him." He is in you and can give you everything you need to get your work done well.

Dear God, please forgive me when I sometimes have
a bad attitude about the work I need to do. I want
to be a happy, hard worker, not a lazy, grumpy one—
and I can do that when I remember You are always
with me and working in me. Thank You! Amen.

HARDWORKING AND HAPPY PART 2

Whatever work you do, do it with all your heart. Do it for the Lord and not for men. Remember that you will get your reward from the Lord. He will give you what you should receive. You are working for the Lord Christ.
COLOSSIANS 3:23–24

No matter what job or task you've been given to do—the ones you like and the ones you sure don't—picture God as your boss or teacher or coach overseeing you. He's your heavenly Father and the very best leader. He loves you more than anyone ever, and He blesses and rewards for good work like no one else can. So do all your work with all your heart! Let God teach you and grow you and give you joy through everything—from math homework to cleaning your room and everything in between. The older you get, the more kinds of jobs and good work God will give you to do. Just watch and see!

· ·

Dear God, please help me do all my work with all my heart— and be happy about it! Remind me that I do work to obey You, and You are the very best boss and heavenly Father. You never stop helping me or loving me. Please bless me and encourage me and keep me working hard for You. Amen.

BEAUTY FROM THE HEART

Do not let your beauty come from the outside. It should not be the way you comb your hair or the wearing of gold or the wearing of fine clothes. Your beauty should come from the inside. It should come from the heart. This is the kind that lasts.

1 PETER 3:3–4

So many things in the world—like on TV and social media and magazines—will try to tell you what beauty is and how to look good. But you will only weaken your courage and confidence if you constantly try to keep up with that nonsense. Instead, focus on what God's Word has to say about real beauty. It comes from the inside, from the heart. You probably know people who look good on the outside but sure don't act beautiful. And you probably know people who don't follow all the beauty and fashion trends who are so truly beautiful from the inside out, with all the goodness and kindness and love they give to others. Which type of person is it better to be—one who focuses on outward beauty or inward beauty? Only one kind of beauty will last. Only one kind of beauty matters to God.

• •

Dear God, help me to focus not on what I look like and what I wear but on beauty that comes from my heart because I love and follow You. Amen.

WHEN SICKNESS IS SCARY

Jesus went over all Galilee. He taught in their places of worship and preached the Good News of the holy nation. He healed all kinds of sickness and disease among the people.

MATTHEW 4:23

Sickness can be so scary, but when you read stories in the Bible of how Jesus healed people, they give courage and confidence, strength and hope. He is always able to heal in any way He chooses. But we also know that He does not always choose to heal here on earth. We all know a friend or loved one who has died. Sometimes God chooses to heal in heaven forever. No matter what sickness you or someone you know is facing, with Jesus no one needs to be afraid. He will help and heal according to His will. He loves and cares for every person and wants everyone to trust in His saving grace.

• •

Dear God, help me not to be afraid of sickness. Thank You for all the ways You help and heal, through medicine and doctors and through prayer and Your power. Thank You that total healing forever from every sickness comes in heaven for all those who trust in Jesus Christ as Savior. Help me to share Your truth and love. Amen.

YOU'RE A STRANGER HERE

Dear friends, your real home is not here on earth. You are strangers here. I ask you to keep away from all the sinful desires of the flesh. These things fight to get hold of your soul.

1 PETER 2:11

Maybe sometimes you feel like a weirdo, trying to be cool in this world but somehow never quite getting there. Guess what? You *should* be a weirdo if you are following close to Jesus! That's a good thing, the best kind of weird. The Bible talks about how we are strangers here on earth because our real home is in heaven. Embrace the weirdness—be happy about it! You have been set apart by God as His child because of your faith in Jesus, and you have the Holy Spirit in you. That doesn't mean you're trying to be a weirdo who is obnoxious or annoying. It just means you will often not fit in with what's popular in the world because so often what is popular in the world is disobedience to God.

• •

Dear God, please help me to be okay with feeling like a stranger here on earth. Remind me that my purpose is not to fit in with the popular crowd. No, my purpose is to follow You in all things here on earth, doing the good things You have planned for me and sharing Your truth and love and the Good News about Jesus. Amen.

LOVING, LOYAL FRIENDSHIP

Jonathan made an agreement with David,
because he loved him as himself.

1 SAMUEL 18:3

Jonathan and David were two of the very best friends in all of history. They had a loyalty and love for each other that can be hard to find in friendships. As you're growing up, friends might come and go. People change as they get older and as situations change. And that's totally normal and okay, even if it's hard to adjust to sometimes. But you can always be praying for a friendship that feels like Jonathan and David's, one that feels almost like your souls are the same (1 Samuel 18:1), one that you know you will have forever even when you're far apart. Focus first on God and your relationship with Him, and then let Him bless you with wonderful friend relationships too.

• •

Dear God, please bless me with the kind of loving and loyal forever friendship that Jonathan and David had. Amen.

ALWAYS GROWING UP

The truth is the Good News. When you heard the truth, you put your trust in Christ. Then God marked you by giving you His Holy Spirit as a promise. The Holy Spirit was given to us as a promise that we will receive everything God has for us. God's Spirit will be with us until God finishes His work of making us complete.

EPHESIANS 1:13–14

Do you think there's a certain age when you're all grown up? What age do you think that is? Yes, at sixteen you can drive, and at eighteen you can vote, and by twenty-two or so many people are done with college and working on their careers. So is it once you're past twenty-two that you're all grown up? In some ways, yes, but let this verse remind you that you're never totally grown up until God finishes His work of making you complete. Every day of your life here on earth, you are meant to keep learning and growing up—up into more maturity and closer relationship with God. You have the Holy Spirit in you as a promise that God is working in and through your life. And one day in heaven you *will* be absolutely perfect and complete.

• •

Dear God, please help me to never stop growing up in relationship with You and in the person You want me to be. Amen.

WHEN YOU'RE ANGRY

If you are angry, do not let it become sin.
Get over your anger before the day is finished.
Do not let the devil start working in your life.
EPHESIANS 4:26–27

It's totally okay to be angry sometimes, like when someone is treating you or others in a cruel or unfair way. But let the Holy Spirit help you to not let that anger become sin. Ask God to help you have wisdom to know what to do with your anger in good ways to bring a solution and an end to whatever has gone wrong. If you don't get over your anger in good and quick ways, it can give the devil a chance to start working in your life instead of letting the Holy Spirit work in your life. No way do you want that!

Dear God, please show me clearly when my anger is bad and when it is good. Please show me what to do with anger in ways that please You and help people love You and love others more. Please help me to never let the devil start working in my life. Amen.

THE TRUTH ABOUT ANGELS

Are not all the angels spirits who work for God?
They are sent out to help those who are to
be saved from the punishment of sin.

HEBREWS 1:14

What do you believe about angels? It's important that what you believe about them comes not from the world's ideas but from the truth in God's Word. This scripture shows you that you can trust that angels absolutely exist. They are spirits who work for God, and they are sent to help all who trust in Jesus as Savior. Isn't that amazing to think about? Don't ever be afraid to ask God to send His angels to help you and rescue you in any kind of trouble.

• •

Dear God, thank You that angels are real and true. Send them to me when I need them. Thank You for the ways You care for me and love me and protect through the help of angels. Amen.

COURAGE AND CONTENTMENT

I am not saying I need anything. I have learned to be happy with whatever I have. I know how to get along with little and how to live when I have much. I have learned the secret of being happy at all times. If I am full of food and have all I need, I am happy. If I am hungry and need more, I am happy. I can do all things because Christ gives me the strength.

PHILIPPIANS 4:11–13

Being content means being happy and satisfied with whatever you have, whether it's a little or lot. Courage and contentment go hand in hand. If you're not worried about what you have or don't have, and if you know you can be happy no matter if you're poor or have plenty, it's easier to be brave. Being content means you're not afraid that you're going to lose something; you're just ready and willing to do what God asks you and happily receive what He gives you.

• •

Dear God, please help me to be content because I remember that I can do all things through Your Son, Jesus. Your Holy Spirit is in me, and I will always have everything I need. Amen.

THE GIFT OF FRIENDSHIP

Two are better than one, because they have good pay for their work. For if one of them falls, the other can help him up. But it is hard for the one who falls when there is no one to lift him up. And if two lie down together, they keep warm. But how can one be warm alone? One man is able to have power over him who is alone, but two can stand against him.

ECCLESIASTES 4:9–12

Friendship is so important to help you be courageous and more! This scripture from Ecclesiastes talks about how friends can help each other and support each other and protect each other and stand against enemies together too. And don't forget how much fun it is to have good friends! That's the extra special blessing on top. God gives us so much joy and fun through good friendships.

• •

Dear God, thank You for the gift of good friendships in my life! Please help my friends and me grow closer together and most of all closer to You. Amen.

BE CAREFUL ABOUT FRIENDSHIPS

He who walks with wise men will be wise, but the one who walks with fools will be destroyed. Trouble follows sinners, but good things will be given to those who are right with God.
PROVERBS 13:20–21

The friends God doesn't want you to have are the ones who will pull you away from obeying Him and having close relationship with Him. So be very careful about choosing who your close friends are. Of course you should be kind and polite to others, but if someone is an unsafe or cruel kind of person who will get you into lots of trouble or make you disobey God, you should totally keep your distance.

• •

Dear God, please give me wisdom about friendship. Please help me keep my distance from anyone who might pull me away from You and into trouble. Please guide me to the friendships that are good for me, ones that will bless me with fun and joy and will support and strengthen my faith in You. Amen.

THE SPIRIT MADE THEM ABLE

The followers of Jesus were all together in one place fifty days after the special religious gathering to remember how the Jews left Egypt. All at once there was a sound from heaven like a powerful wind. It filled the house where they were sitting. Then they saw tongues which were divided that looked like fire. These came down on each one of them. They were all filled with the Holy Spirit. Then they began to speak in other languages which the Holy Spirit made them able to speak.

ACTS 2:1–4

Can you imagine being there with the ancient followers of Jesus? What would it have been like to see tongues of fire coming down on you? Probably kinda terrifying, right? But God is good, and He was doing a good thing. He was filling His followers with the Holy Spirit in a powerful way to let them speak in other languages so that all the people gathered there from all around the world could learn about the one true God and how He saves people from sin through His Son, Jesus. Incredible!

• •

Dear God, You are all-powerful, and I believe You can do absolutely anything! Keep spreading Your truth all over the world! Please use me to help. Amen.

BUILD YOUR LIFE ON THE ROCK

You are God's building also. Through God's loving-favor to me, I laid the stones on which the building was to be built. I did it like one who knew what he was doing. Now another person is building on it. Each person who builds must be careful how he builds on it. Jesus Christ is the Stone on which other stones for the building must be laid.

1 CORINTHIANS 3:9–11

The next time you're at the beach or playing in the sand somewhere, think of this scripture. You know that nothing built on sand stays stable. Waves and wind can destroy it in an instant. Your life can't be stable either if you only build it on sand, meaning the false, weak ways of the world. You must build your life on Jesus the Rock and all the truth we are given in His Word. The Holy Spirit is always with you to help you build on the Rock. Let Him lead you as you build your life!

• •

Dear God, please build my life on the strong and steady Rock of Jesus. Amen.

WHEN YOU FEEL GRUMPY

Loving-favor and loving-kindness and peace are ours as we live in truth and love. These come from God the Father and from the Lord Jesus Christ, Who is the Son of the Father.

2 JOHN 1:3

When do you feel most grumpy? Is it in the mornings just after you wake up? After a rough day at school? Before bed when you're super tired but don't actually want to admit it? It's hard to show kindness and love in those grumpy times. But when we feel like we don't have any kindness and love to give, we need to remember that God always does. And through His Holy Spirit within us we can choose to act in kind and loving ways even when we don't feel like it. The next time you're in a grumpy mood, stop and remember this scripture. Loving-kindness and peace are yours because your heavenly Father gives them to you.

- -

Dear God, I don't always feel like being nice, but I can focus on Your kindness and love that are in me through Your Holy Spirit. Help me to think and act on those good things, not on my own grumpy moods. Amen.

BE CAREFUL HOW YOU ACT

When you are around people who do not know God, be careful how you act. Even if they talk against you as wrong-doers, in the end they will give thanks to God for your good works when Christ comes again.

1 PETER 2:12

Do you think much about your reputation, how your actions and words affect what others think about you? Even when you're young, you *should* think about it! God's view of you matters most of all, but He also wants you to act and speak in ways that will help others want to know Him. If you care about your reputation and always strive to make it a good one (knowing that, of course, you'll make mistakes sometimes), then even if someone tries to say bad things about you, no one will believe them because your life will have shown mostly truth and goodness.

• •

Dear God, help me to care what You think most of all but also to remember that what others think of me—my reputation—matters too. I want my words and actions, my whole life, to point to Your goodness, truth, and love so that others will know You and accept Jesus Christ as their Savior. Amen.

DON'T GIVE IN

Now the snake was more able to fool others than any animal of the field which the Lord God had made. He said to the woman, "Did God say that you should not eat from any tree in the garden?"

GENESIS 3:1

Has anyone ever tempted you to do what you knew was wrong? Maybe there was a substitute teacher at school one day, and a classmate said something like this: "Did our regular teacher really say we aren't allowed to do whatever we want? Let's have fun and confuse the sub!" It might seem like no big deal until your regular teacher finds out what you did and you find yourself in big trouble. Temptations today are the same kinds of ways the devil, disguised as a snake in the Garden of Eden, convinced the first people to sin. When you know what is good and right and true, don't let anyone try to make you question it and convince you to sin and disobey.

. . . .

Dear God, please help me to remember how the devil convinced Adam and Eve to sin and how that sin continues still today. Thank You for Your grace that covers my sin, but please help me to do my very best to obey You and not listen and give in to evil and temptation. Amen.

FULL OF THE HOLY SPIRIT AND FAITH

*The news of this came to the church in Jerusalem. They
sent Barnabas to Antioch. When he got there and saw
how good God had been to them, he was full of joy. He
told them to be true and faithful to the Lord. Barnabas
was a good man and full of the Holy Spirit and faith.
And many people became followers of the Lord.*

ACTS 11:22–24

The name Barnabas is a fun one to remember, and he is a great
role model from the Bible to remember too! He was "a good man
and full of the Holy Spirit and faith." Likewise, you should want
to be called "a good girl and full of the Holy Spirit and faith."
Because of Barnabas's good life and great example of following
Jesus, many other people became followers of Jesus. How cool
if many others become followers of Jesus because of your good
life and faith in Jesus too!

• •

**Dear Jesus, I want to always be filled with the Holy Spirit
and faith. I want to live such a good life as Your follower that
others will see my example and want to follow You too! Amen.**

GO-TO SCRIPTURE

*For God did not give us a spirit of fear. He gave us
a spirit of power and of love and of a good mind.*

2 TIMOTHY 1:7

When you feel afraid, what helps comfort you and make you feel safe? Bible verses you've memorized should be a top go-to, like 2 Timothy 1:7, reminding you God has given you a spirit of power and love and with a good mind to defeat any spirit of fear. Another to memorize and repeat is Psalm 56:3–4: "When I am afraid, I will trust in You. I praise the Word of God. I have put my trust in God. I will not be afraid." God's Word is powerful to help us in any scary situation.

• •

**Dear God, thank You for Your Word that I can memorize
and repeat when I need to focus on Your power and
love. Please help me in any situation where I feel scared.
Remind me that nothing and no one can ever defeat
me because You are within me through Your Holy Spirit.
You take good care of me, no matter what. Amen.**

A WOMAN WHO SPOKE FOR GOD

Deborah, a woman who spoke for God, was judging Israel at that time. She would sit under the tree of Deborah between Ramah and Bethel in the hill country of Ephraim. And the people of Israel came to her to find out what was right or wrong.

JUDGES 4:4–5

Wow, can you imagine what it was like to be Deborah of the Bible? She was the only female judge of the people of Israel. Back in Bible times, when most women were considered far less valuable than men, that was a really big deal that she was in such a high position. God surely was helping her to be courageous and even more—she was a "woman who spoke for God." Let Deborah inspire you to be a girl who speaks for God and grow up to be a woman who speaks for God. Let God help you know right from wrong, and let Him lead you and speak through you to others who need to hear His truth and love.

• •

Dear God, help me to be like Deborah, speaking for You and knowing right from wrong. Amen.

WHEN GOD'S FACE SHINES ON YOU

"May the Lord bring good to you and keep you. May the Lord make His face shine upon you, and be kind to you."
NUMBERS 6:24–25

Do you ever think about if God's face is shining on you? What do you think that means? Do you ever look at someone and feel like your face goes into a big beaming smile because you love them so much? Do you ever look at a project you've done or think of a game you've won and feel a big beaming smile of pride in your accomplishment? Think of those things when you think of God making His face shine on you. It's with great love and pride that He smiles on you because you're His child. How have you seen that in your life, and how has He shown great kindness to you? It's wonderful to think about these things regularly to fill up with gratitude and remind yourself how God has been kind and will continue to be kind when you're following Him.

• •

**Dear God, I love picturing Your face shining on me.
Thank You so much for all Your love and kindness
to me. Keep me close to You. Amen.**

LESSONS FROM THE TOWER OF BABEL PART I

"Come, let us build a city for ourselves, with a tower that touches the heavens. Let us make a name for ourselves, or else we may be sent everywhere over the whole earth."

GENESIS 11:4

The story of the Tower of Babel seems to start out like a good idea. The people wanted to work together on a big project—a really big one. They wanted their tower to practically reach heaven. The problem was, they had way too much pride in themselves and their own talents and abilities. They weren't thinking about God and His perfect plans and the fact that He is the One who gives all talents and abilities. God still loved the people, but He knew their plans were wrong and full of pride. So God ruined their plans. He gave them different languages so they couldn't understand one another.

• •

Dear God, teach me from the stories about ancient people in Your Word. Show me the good lessons You want me to learn from them for today. Amen.

LESSONS FROM THE TOWER OF BABEL PART 2

"Come, let Us go down and mix up their language so they will not understand what each other says." So the Lord sent them everywhere over the whole earth. And they stopped building the city. So the name of the city was Babel, because there the Lord mixed up the language of the whole earth. The Lord sent the people everywhere over the whole earth.

GENESIS 11:7–9

Like He did in the story of the Tower of Babel, God might ruin our plans sometimes too. Sometimes that's to keep us safe or to keep us on His plan, and sometimes it's because our plan was too full of pride. We have to constantly ask Him to help us want to obey His perfect plans for us and give Him all the praise for the wonderful talents, abilities, and blessings that come from Him.

• •

Dear God, please help me to focus on wanting what Your perfect plans are for me. Please ruin any plans that would be bad for me. Help me not to have pride in myself but instead have gratitude for the talents and abilities You have given me. You know me and love me and always want what's best for me. Amen.

FEED YOUR BODY, HEART, MIND, AND SOUL

Jesus said, "It is written, 'Man is not to live on bread only. Man is to live by every word that God speaks.' "

MATTHEW 4:4

If you don't eat all day, what happens? You feel awful, right? Your stomach growls and hurts, and maybe your head hurts too. You feel tired and weak. We all need food, and we can't last very long without it. Remember that Jesus talked about us not just needing food to eat but also needing the truth of God's words. We find them in the Bible. So just like we usually feed our bodies with breakfast, lunch, and dinner (and probably some yummy snacks in between!), we need to feed our hearts and minds and souls with God's good truth to strengthen and nourish and encourage us.

• •

Dear God, help me to remember that listening to and learning from You, especially through Your Word, is as important to my heart, mind, and soul as food is to my body. Amen.

GOD DID NOT LEAVE THEM

"You are a forgiving God. You are kind and loving, slow to anger, and full of loving-kindness. You did not leave them. . . . They spoke sinful words against You. But You, in Your great loving-kindness, did not leave them in the desert. . . . You gave Your good Spirit to teach them. You did not keep Your bread from heaven from their mouths. And You gave them water when they were thirsty. For forty years You kept them alive in the desert and gave them everything they needed."

NEHEMIAH 9:17–21

Let this scripture remind you how patient and good our God is, even when His people treat Him badly. He is forgiving and kind and loving. He provides for His people and gives His Holy Spirit to teach them. This scripture might be about ancient times and ancient people, but you can apply the truth in it to your own life today.

• •

Dear God, thank You for loving Your people, including me, so well. Please forgive me when I treat You badly and sin against You. Thank You for being so patient. Thank You that You are always willing to forgive me and You never stop loving or providing for me. Amen.

THE BATTLE IS NOT YOURS

"The Lord says to you, 'Do not be afraid or troubled because of these many men. For the battle is not yours but God's. . . . You will not need to fight in this battle. Just stand still in your places and see the saving power of the Lord work for you, O Judah and Jerusalem.' Do not be afraid or troubled. Go out against them tomorrow, for the Lord is with you."

2 CHRONICLES 20:15, 17

When a problem in your life seems way too overwhelming, think of this Bible story. God told His people, who were up against a great enemy army, that the battle was not theirs but His. He told them they wouldn't even need to fight but just to stand and watch His saving power work for them. Sometimes all you need to do is just stand strong in your faith and watch what God does to rescue you from trouble.

• •

Dear God, show when I just need to stand still and strong and let You do all the fighting for me. Thank You! Amen.

RUN TO WIN

You know that only one person gets a crown for being in a race even if many people run. You must run so you will win the crown. Everyone who runs in a race does many things so his body will be strong. He does it to get a crown that will soon be worth nothing, but we work for a crown that will last forever. In the same way, I run straight for the place at the end of the race. I fight to win.

1 CORINTHIANS 9:24–26

Whether we like to run or not, the Bible says we're all in a race! And heaven is where we'll get our prize. It will be an extraordinary prize—one that will last forever. How we run our race here on earth matters, so we should do our very best in the way we live and use the gifts God has given us to serve Him and others. We should do the good things He has planned for us and help others love Jesus and give God all the glory!

• •

Dear God, please remind me every day that I'm in a wonderful race You've put me in here on earth. Please help me to run well, looking ahead to a perfect forever prize in heaven. Amen.

WHAT NOT TO DO AND WHERE NOT TO GO

They went through the countries of Phrygia and Galatia. The Holy Spirit kept them from preaching the Word of God in the countries of Asia. When they came to the city of Mysia, they tried to go on to the city of Bithynia but the Holy Spirit would not let them go. From Mysia they went down to the city of Troas.

ACTS 16:6–8

Paul and Timothy were good friends and followers of Jesus who let the Holy Spirit lead them. And the Holy Spirit stopped them from doing certain things and going certain places. You are filled with the Holy Spirit too, and sometimes the Holy Spirit will stop you from doing certain things and help you know what *not* to do. This can be to protect you and teach you and guide you where God wants you to be.

• •

Dear God, as You show me the good things You have planned for me, please always also help me listen to Your Holy Spirit about what not to do and where not to go. Amen.

EVERY MORNING

But this I remember, and so I have hope. It is because of the Lord's loving-kindness that we are not destroyed for His loving-pity never ends. It is new every morning. He is so very faithful. "The Lord is my share." says my soul, "so I have hope in Him." The Lord is good to those who wait for Him, to the one who looks for Him. It is good that one should be quiet and wait for the saving power of the Lord.

LAMENTATIONS 3:21–26

When you wake up on a new day, how do you feel? Hopefully you've gotten some good sleep and you have a fresh start, no matter what happened yesterday. God's Word talks about how God's love and mercy are new to us every morning. As you open your eyes and climb out of bed, think of this scripture and let it give you courage and hope for whatever you're facing each day.

• •

Dear God, thank You for being so loving and kind and faithful to me! Thank You for brand-new days with fresh starts. I trust in You and Your power today and every day. Amen.

THE FOOLISH SON

*"The son got up and went to his father. While he was yet
a long way off, his father saw him. The father was full of
loving-pity for him. He ran and threw his arms around him
and kissed him. The son said to him, 'Father, I have sinned
against heaven and against you. . . .' But the father said. . .
'Bring the calf that is fat and kill it. Let us eat and be glad.
For my son was dead and now he is alive again. He was lost
and now he is found. Let us eat and have a good time.' "*
LUKE 15:20–24

Do you ever feel like you've messed up so badly you might never
be forgiven? Like you might need to run away and never come
back? Then let the story Jesus told of the foolish son help you remember that God loves you *no matter what.* Just like the father in
the story welcomed back his son (with so much love and even a
party!), God your heavenly Father will always welcome you back if
you turn away from your mistakes and run into His forgiving arms.

• •

**Dear heavenly Father, thank You for Your
endless, forgiving love for me. Amen.**

PRAISE HIM!

Praise the Lord! Praise God in His holy place! Praise Him in the heavens of His power! Praise Him for His great works! Praise Him for all His greatness! Praise Him with the sound of a horn. Praise Him with harps. Praise Him with timbrels and dancing. Praise Him with strings and horns. Praise Him with loud sounds. Praise Him with loud and clear sounds. Let everything that has breath praise the Lord. Praise the Lord!

PSALM 150

Do you see a theme in this scripture? What are we supposed to do? *Praise the Lord*—everywhere, for everything, in all kinds of ways! We can be courageous and more when we are full of praise to God because constantly praising means we are constantly aware of God's greatness. When we focus on that greatness and how He loves and cares for us, we have absolutely nothing to fear.

• •

Dear God, yes, I praise You! You are awesome! You are greater than any problem or enemy I will ever face. I have nothing to fear when I'm praising and trusting You! Amen.

REMEMBER JONAH

The Lord sent a big fish to swallow Jonah, and he was in the stomach of the fish for three days and three nights.

JONAH 1:17

Have you ever had consequences for your actions that seemed totally crazy unfair? Imagine what Jonah must have felt like when he was sitting inside the belly of a big fish! Yes, he ran away from God, but Jonah might have been thinking, *Really, God? This is super weird and disgusting, and it really stinks in here! Couldn't I have learned my lesson not to disobey You in some other way?* But sometimes God wants to get our attention in a dramatic way to say, *"It's so super important that you obey My plans for you. They are the best plans, and they're for your good and the good of others."* When you feel God asking you to follow His plan, remember not to be like Jonah. Don't go your own way instead. You sure don't want God to have to get your attention and give you consequences in an extremely weird or hard way, like in the belly of a fish!

• •

Dear God, help me to remember Jonah. Remind me how important it is to follow You, even when I feel like I'd rather go my own way. Amen.

UNSTOPPABLE

"But before all this happens, men will take hold of you and make it very hard for you. They will give you over to the places of worship and to the prisons. They will bring you in front of kings and the leaders of the people. This will all be done to you because of Me. This will be a time for you to tell about Me. Do not think about what you will say ahead of time. For I will give you wisdom in what to say and I will help you say it. Those who are against you will not be able to stop you or say you are wrong."

LUKE 21:12–15

Jesus warned His followers that they would find themselves in dangerous trouble because they loved and obeyed and preached about Him. But He sure didn't tell them to give up. He told them to stay strong and not worry, not even about what they would say. He promised to give them wisdom and words and help so that they would be unstoppable.

Dear Jesus, if I find myself in trouble or danger for following You, I never want to give up my faith or stop telling others about You. Help me to stay strong and trust that You will give me wisdom for exactly what I need to do and say. Amen.

GOD LIGHTS YOUR DARKNESS AND COVERS YOU WITH STRENGTH

You make my lamp bright. The Lord my God lights my darkness. With Your help I can go against many soldiers. With my God I can jump over a wall. . . . The Word of the Lord has stood the test. He is a covering for all who go to Him for a safe place. For Who is God, but the Lord? And who is a rock except our God? It is God Who covers me with strength and makes my way perfect. . . . He teaches me how to fight.

PSALM 18:28–33, 35

Wow, when you read verses from Psalms like these, they can help you feel powerful enough to do anything at all because it is God's power working in you through the Holy Spirit. At times when you feel afraid and discouraged, worried and weak, think about how much time you've been spending in the Bible and in prayer. Has it been enough?

• •

Dear God, please help me not to forget how much You strengthen and empower me when I regularly focus on the truth in Your Word and spend time praying to You. Amen.

THE WAY YOU LIVE AND WORK

Live and work without pride. Be gentle and kind. Do not be hard on others. Let love keep you from doing that. Work hard to live together as one by the help of the Holy Spirit.
EPHESIANS 4:2–3

We can apply these words from Paul in the Bible to all kinds of situations in our lives today. First in our homes with our families. Also in relationships with friends. Definitely among people at church. How about in your activities like sports teams and bands and dance and art groups? What if every person in all these situations acted without pride and always with gentleness and kindness and love? What if everyone lived and worked together as one by letting the Holy Spirit of God help them? Wow—everything would be amazing! None of us can follow this verse perfectly, but if we do our best at it, then we will inspire others to do their best at it too.

• •

Dear God, help me by Your Holy Spirit to work hard to live together as one—without pride and with gentleness, kindness, and love—in my relationships and activities and with my family and friends.

EVERYONE WAS HEALED

They ran through all the country bringing people who were sick on their beds to Jesus. Wherever He went, they would lay the sick people in the streets in the center of town where people gather. They begged Him that they might touch the bottom of His coat. Everyone who did was healed. This happened in the towns and in the cities and in the country where He went.

MARK 6:55–56

Can you imagine how sad it would be to see so many sick people lying in the streets of a town? But then how amazing to see Jesus heal them with even just a touch to the bottom of His coat! Our minds can barely comprehend it. We don't have Jesus with us today to witness this in person, but we do have the Holy Spirit He sent to us. The same power of God in the Holy Spirit is able to heal and do anything God chooses.

• •

Dear Jesus, I wish I could have seen Your life here on earth in person, but I trust in Your healing power. I trust the Holy Spirit within me is also able to heal and do absolutely anything according to God's will. May Your will be done in all things. Amen.

THE TROUBLE OF THIS WORLD

The power is from God. It is not from ourselves. We are
pressed on every side, but we still have room to move.
We are often in much trouble, but we never give up.
People make it hard for us, but we are not left alone.
We are knocked down, but we are not destroyed.

2 CORINTHIANS 4:7–9

Having the power of God in us through the Holy Spirit doesn't mean He makes everything easy. In fact, Jesus said, "In the world you will have much trouble. But take hope! I have power over the world!" (John 16:33). What trouble are you struggling with in life right now? Whatever it is, remember that even on the worst days when you're "pressed on every side" or in a lot of trouble or knocked down or being given a hard time, you don't ever have to give up. You are never alone or destroyed. God has power over all, in good times and bad. Keep trusting and depending on Him.

• •

Dear God, I don't like the trouble of this world, but I know
You will never leave me to face it alone. You will help me to
never give up, no matter how bad the trouble seems. Amen.

BIG LOVE FOR GOD'S WORD

O, how I love Your Law! It is what I think about all through the day. Your Word makes me wiser than those who hate me, for it is always with me. I have better understanding than all my teachers because I think about Your Law. I have a better understanding than those who are old because I obey Your Word. I have kept my feet from every sinful way so that I may keep Your Word. I have not turned away from Your Law, for You Yourself have taught me. How sweet is Your Word to my taste! It is sweeter than honey to my mouth! I get understanding from Your Law and so I hate every false way.

PSALM 119:97–104

This scripture from Psalms is how we should think of and praise God for the Bible! We should have such big love for God's Word. We are so blessed to have it and to follow it!

• •

Dear God, help me to value Your Word all day, every day of my life. Remind me of this psalm. I sing and pray it to You with all my heart. Amen.

GOD SENT HIS ANGEL

"Daniel, servant of the living God, has your God, Whom you always serve, been able to save you from the lions?" Then Daniel said to the king, "O king, live forever! My God sent His angel and shut the lions' mouths. They have not hurt me."

DANIEL 6:20–22

God could have made Daniel fly out of the den. He could have killed the lions. He could have made the king switch places with Daniel. He could have saved Daniel in any way He chose. But God sent His angel to shut the mouths of the lions. (Do you ever wonder if Daniel was able to pet them and make friends once their mouths were shut? What a fun thought!) God can send His angels to help and rescue you at any moment, for any reason, in ways you may never even realize.

• •

Dear God, help me to remember You have angels You can send to help me anywhere, anytime. That gives me courage and confidence and boldness to face any problem or challenge or danger or fear that might come my way. Amen.

ANANIAS AND SAPPHIRA'S SAD STORY

A man by the name of Ananias and his wife, Sapphira, sold some land. He kept back part of the money for himself. His wife knew it also. The other part he took to the missionaries. Peter said to Ananias, "Why did you let Satan fill your heart? He made you lie to the Holy Spirit."

ACTS 5:1–3

Spoiler alert! The story of Ananias and Sapphira in the Bible is a tough one to read because of the sad ending—they both die because of a mistake. A big mistake of lying to God. The story teaches us a lesson on how important honesty is, especially honesty to God. As you're growing up, are you a girl who values telling the truth in all things? Even in the little things? The little things become the big things, and even now if you value the truth like God does, you'll grow up to be trustworthy and honorable, full of integrity that pleases God.

• •

Dear God, help me to love the truth like You do. Help me never to lie. If I make mistakes, help me to admit them right away and work to make things right. I want to be trustworthy and full of integrity, both now and when I'm all grown up. Amen.

JESUS IS EVERYTHING!

Be careful that no one changes your mind and faith by much learning and big sounding ideas. Those things are what men dream up. They are always trying to make new religions. These leave out Christ. For Christ is not only God-like, He is God in human flesh. When you have Christ, you are complete. He is the head over all leaders and powers.

COLOSSIANS 2:8–10

Jesus is everything! This scripture says when you have Him, you are complete. It's as simple as that. We don't need a lot of big-sounding ideas, and we sure don't need any false religions. We just need to trust in who Jesus is and what He did and share the Good News about Him to everyone, everywhere in all the ways we can.

• •

Dear Jesus, You are everything. You make me complete when I know You as Savior because then the Holy Spirit lives within me to lead and guide me. Amen.

DON'T BE LAZY

In the name of the Lord Jesus, keep away from any Christian who is lazy and who does not do what we taught you. You know you should follow the way of life we lived when we were with you. We worked hard while we were there. We did not eat anyone's food without paying for it. We worked hard night and day so none of you would have to give us anything. . . . When we were with you, we told you that if a man does not work, he should not eat. We hear that some are not working. But they are spending their time trying to see what others are doing. Our words to such people are that they should be quiet and go to work.

2 THESSALONIANS 3:6–8, 10–12

We sure do need some time in life to just rest and relax and have fun. That's wonderful! But we have to be careful that we don't like all that *too* much. We don't want to become lazy. What does this scripture tell you about being lazy compared to being a hard worker? What should you strive to be?

• •

Dear God, please bless me with good times to rest and relax and have fun like I should, but also help me to never become lazy. Show me the good work You want me to do and help me to find joy in it. Amen.

LOVING THE POOR AND NEEDY

" 'I was hungry and you gave Me food to eat. I was thirsty and you gave Me water to drink. I was a stranger and you gave Me a room. I had no clothes and you gave Me clothes to wear. I was sick and you cared for Me. I was in prison and you came to see Me.' "Then those that are right with God will say, 'Lord, when did we see You hungry and feed You? When did we see You thirsty and give You a drink? When did we see You a stranger and give You a room? When did we see You had no clothes and we gave You clothes? And when did we see You sick or in prison and we came to You?' Then the King will say, 'For sure, I tell you, because you did it to one of the least of My brothers, you have done it to Me.' "

MATTHEW 25:35–40

We can't ever forget how important it is to help people who are in need. Jesus said that serving them is like serving Him. When we show love to the poor and needy, we are showing love to Jesus.

• •

Dear Jesus, I want to serve You and love You by serving and loving others. Please show me those who need my help. Amen.

GOD CAN DO ALL THINGS

Jesus said to His followers, "For sure, I tell you, it will be hard for a rich man to get into the holy nation of heaven. Again I tell you, it is easier for a camel to go through the eye of a needle than for a rich man to get into the holy nation of heaven." When His followers heard this, they could not understand it. They said, "Then who can be saved from the punishment of sin?" Jesus looked at them and said, "This cannot be done by men. But with God all things can be done."
MATTHEW 19:23–26

Maybe you are praying for loved ones to trust Jesus as their Savior, but they just refuse to admit their need for Him. It might seem absolutely impossible, but keep on praying for them and loving them anyway. Remember this scripture that with God, all things can be done, even the totally impossible.

• •

Dear God, I pray for my friends and loved ones who seem so against trusting You as Savior. Help me to remember that nothing is impossible for You! Amen.

BE TOUGH AND HAPPY

"Those who have it very hard for doing right are happy, because the holy nation of heaven is theirs. You are happy when people act and talk in a bad way to you and make it very hard for you and tell bad things and lies about you because you trust in Me. Be glad and full of joy because your reward will be much in heaven."
MATTHEW 5:10–12

It's not always easy to faithfully follow Jesus in this world. At times people will make things harder for us, talk badly about us, and even lie about us because we love and follow Jesus. When it happens to you, remember this scripture and be tough and happy. God sees and knows and cares—and He will reward us in heaven for every hard thing we go through, every mean thing said against us, here on earth. And in heaven nothing will take our joy away. We'll never have any hard times or hear any mean words ever again.

• •

Dear God, help me to be courageous and tough and even happy when I'm going through hard times and hear mean words because I'm trying to do right and follow Jesus. With Your help, I'll never give up. Amen.

WITH JUST A LITTLE LUNCH

"There is a boy here who has five loaves of barley bread and two small fish. What is that for so many people?" Jesus said, "Have the people sit down." There was much grass in that place. About five thousand men sat down. Jesus took the loaves and gave thanks. Then He gave the bread to those who were sitting down. The fish were given out the same way. The people had as much as they wanted. When they were filled, Jesus said to His followers, "Gather up the pieces that are left. None will be wasted." The followers gathered the pieces together. Twelve baskets were filled with pieces of barley bread. These were left after all the people had eaten. The people saw the powerful work Jesus had done. They said, "It is true! This is the One Who speaks for God Who is to come into the world."

JOHN 6:9–14

What a miracle God did with just a little lunch from a little boy! Remember this story anytime you might be wondering why you matter and what God can do with you. He loves you, and His power is working in you to do any good work He has planned.

• •

Dear Jesus, You can take the smallest things and create the biggest miracles! You are amazing. Amen.

DON'T MAKE GOD SAD

*Do not make God's Holy Spirit have sorrow for the way you
live. . . . Put out of your life all these things: bad feelings about
other people, anger, temper, loud talk, bad talk which hurts other
people, and bad feelings which hurt other people. You must be
kind to each other. Think of the other person. Forgive other people
just as God forgave you because of Christ's death on the cross.*
EPHESIANS 4:30–32

With the Holy Spirit in you, God can help you make all the best choices
in life that guide you in good things and bless you and bless others.
But when you make bad choices in life, there are consequences—
and we literally make God sad. He loves us no matter what, but
we can still make Him sad, and we can still create hardship and
problems for ourselves when we behave badly. So do your best to
follow the scripture above—put out of your life bad feelings about
others, anger, bad talk, and so on. Put into your life more kindness,
forgiveness, and caring for others—the things that make God happy.
These things will make you and others happy too!

**Dear God, I don't want to make You sad. Help me to
make good choices in the way I live and the way I treat
others—choices that obey You, honor You, and point
others to knowing and loving You too. Amen.**

THEY FEARED GOD

Then the king of Egypt spoke to the Hebrew nurses. The name of one was Shiphrah. The name of the other was Puah. He said, "When you are helping the Hebrew women to give birth, and see the baby before the mother does, if it is a son, kill him. But if it is a daughter, let her live." But the nurses feared God. They did not do what the king of Egypt told them. They let the boys live.

EXODUS 1:15–17

Sometimes it takes courage and more to know when it's actually good to disobey—like Shiphrah and Puah did when they refused to kill new baby boys as the king of Egypt had demanded. These ladies knew it was evil to end the lives of helpless babies. They feared, or respected, God. Like brave Shiphrah and Puah, we need wisdom from God to know when and how to disobey rulers when they are acting with evil and forcing others to act with evil too.

• •

Dear God, please give me the wisdom and courage I need to know when and how to help stop evil. Amen.

COURAGEOUS AND CLEVER

The time came when she could hide him no longer. So she took a basket made from grass, and covered it with tar and put the child in it. And she set it in the grass by the side of the Nile. His sister stayed to watch and find out what would happen to him. . . . His sister said to Pharaoh's daughter, "Should I go and call a nurse from the Hebrew women to nurse the child for you?" Pharaoh's daughter said to her, "Go." So the girl went and called the child's mother.

EXODUS 2:3–4, 7–8

Moses' mother, Jochebed, and her daughter, Miriam, were courageous and clever when they made a plan to save baby Moses from being killed by the Egyptians. It was such a good plan that Moses ended up being raised as royalty. Mostly, it was such a good plan because God was working even bigger plans through it.

• •

Dear God, please help me to be both courageous and clever. Give me good ideas and plans that help Your great big plans to be done and bring all praise to You! Amen.

WHEN YOU'RE TEMPTED TO BE SNEAKY

Achan answered Joshua, saying, "It is true. I have sinned against the Lord, the God of Israel. . . . I saw 200 pieces of silver, and a large piece of gold as heavy as fifty pieces of silver. I had a desire for them and took them. See, they are hidden in the ground inside my tent, with the silver under it."

JOSHUA 7:20–21

Have you ever been tempted to take something that wasn't yours and lie about it? Maybe when you were younger you really wanted a friend's little toy and she already had a bunch of them, so you just snuck one into your pocket. Or maybe all those candy bars at the store looked yummy, so you grabbed one under your shirt when no one was looking. Is a toy as fun as it should be when it's taken in a dishonest way? Hopefully not. Does candy taste as good as it should when it's eaten in a sneaky, stealing way? It shouldn't. We should love being honest because God loves honesty. We should learn from the story of Achan in the Bible, who brought great trouble on himself and his people because he took things he shouldn't have.

· ·

Dear God, please help me not to be greedy and sneaky and dishonest. If I mess up, please forgive me and help me to make things right. Thank You for Your love and grace. Amen.

STAY ON A STRAIGHT PATH

Teach me to do Your will, for You are my God. Let Your good Spirit lead me on a straight path. Give me new life, O Lord, because of Your name. Bring me out of trouble because You are right and good.

PSALM 143:10–11

Do you let God lead you on a straight path? What does it look like in your life to be on a straight path—at home and at school? With your siblings and friends? In your activities and hobbies? Keep asking God to lead you every day. Let Him guide you out of trouble if you're in it, and let Him keep you out of trouble. Let Him give you the best kind of life because You trust and follow Him.

• •

Dear God, I want Your Spirit inside me to lead me on a straight path. Help me to stay out of trouble and follow You no matter what because You are always right and good. Amen.

HOLD TO THE TRUTH

*False teaching is like the wind. False teachers try
everything possible to make people believe a lie, but
we are to hold to the truth with love in our hearts.
We are to grow up and be more like Christ.*

EPHESIANS 4:14–15

Every day it seems there are more confusing things in the world, more people telling us that it's not loving or kind to tell the truth about Jesus and the truth found in God's Word. Ask the Holy Spirit in you to give you wisdom to know what is false teaching and what is not. Ask Him to help you hold on tight to God's truth while keeping love in your heart to share it with others.

• •

Dear God, please help me to never be blown around by the wind of false teaching. Keep me firmly stable in Your truth. Keep Your love in my heart as I share Your truth with others. Amen.

REAL LOVE AND PEACE

*Now that we have been made right with God
by putting our trust in Him, we have peace with Him.
It is because of what our Lord Jesus Christ did for us.
By putting our trust in God, He has given us His loving-
favor and has received us. We are happy for the hope
we have of sharing the shining-greatness of God.*

ROMANS 5:1–2

Peace. Love. Those are popular, powerful, wonderful words! The world around you will try to tell you what they mean, but the absolute truth about them is always in God's Word. Real peace is knowing you are made right with God because of Jesus Christ taking away your sin on the cross. And real love is the love of God that comes into our hearts through His Holy Spirit.

• •

**Dear God, please help me to always know what
peace and love really mean because I learn about
them from You and Your Word! Amen.**

STAND UP AND SPEAK

At that time some men who preached God's Word came to Antioch and told what was going to happen. They were from Jerusalem. One of them was Agabus. The Holy Spirit told him to stand up and speak. He told them there would be very little food to eat over all the world. This happened when Claudius was leader of the country. The Christians agreed that each one should give what money he could to help the Christians living in Judea. They did this and sent it to the church leaders with Barnabas and Saul.

ACTS 11:27–30

When the Holy Spirit told Agabus to stand up and speak, he did it. And because he was obedient, he was able to help take care of other Christians who might soon have been starving without food to eat. When you obey the Holy Spirit, God helps you and helps others through you too. Always be listening for and ready to do anything God asks through His Holy Spirit within you.

• •

Dear God, I want to obey and stand up and speak if You ask me to, just like Agabus did. Help me to listen well for You. Amen.

KEEP ON PRAYING

You must pray at all times as the Holy Spirit leads
you to pray. Pray for the things that are needed.
You must watch and keep on praying.
EPHESIANS 6:18

It's great to have set prayer times to focus intently on prayer, but don't ever forget that the Bible says to pray "at all times as the Holy Spirit leads you." Another scripture says, "Never stop praying. In everything give thanks" (1 Thessalonians 5:17–18). With God, you can never talk too much! Pray to Him and praise Him in your mind every moment of every day and especially as the Holy Spirit leads you. Ask Him for His help for yourself and for others in all situations. Praise Him and thank Him for who He is and for what He does. Tell Him about the needs of others and your own needs. Let Him be your most trusted listening ear and your constant best friend.

Dear God, don't let me forget that I can pray to You at all times—no matter when it is, where I am, and who I'm with. Thank You for loving me and wanting to lead me and help me in every part of my life. Amen.

ALWAYS WATCHING OVER YOU

I will lift up my eyes to the mountains. Where will my help come from? My help comes from the Lord, Who made heaven and earth. He will not let your feet go out from under you. He Who watches over you will not sleep. Listen, He Who watches over Israel will not close his eyes or sleep. The Lord watches over you. The Lord is your safe cover at your right hand. The sun will not hurt you during the day and the moon will not hurt you during the night. The Lord will keep you from all that is sinful. He will watch over your soul. The Lord will watch over your coming and going, now and forever.

PSALM 121

Even as much as your mom and dad and other grown-ups in your life love and watch over you, they can never do as good a job as God can. He is not human like us. He doesn't get tired; He never needs to sleep. Whenever you need help with anything, look up to remember that the Creator of mountains and heavens and earth is right within you through His Spirit.

• •

Dear God, You are my constant helper and hero. Thank You for always watching over me, now and forever. Amen.

GOD GIVES GOOD THINGS

"Ask, and what you are asking for will be given to you. Look, and what you are looking for you will find. Knock, and the door you are knocking on will be opened to you. Everyone who asks receives what he asks for. Everyone who looks finds what he is looking for. Everyone who knocks has the door opened to him. What man among you would give his son a stone if he should ask for bread? Or if he asks for a fish, would he give him a snake? You are bad and you know how to give good things to your children. How much more will your Father in heaven give good things to those who ask Him?"

MATTHEW 7:7–11

Sometimes your parents might get tired of you talking and asking for things, but God does not. He's your wonderful heavenly Dad! Keep talking to Him about everything. He loves you and wants to hear from you. He loves to give you good things.

Dear God, thank You for wanting me to talk to You and ask You for good things in my life. Please bless me in the ways You know are best for me. Amen.

LET YOUR MOUTH SPEAK THE TRUTH

*What is right will come from my lips. For my mouth
will speak the truth. My lips hate wrong-doing. All
the words of my mouth are right and good. There
is nothing in them that is against the truth.*

PROVERBS 8:6–8

Truth matters in all things, so we should make Proverbs 8:6–8 our goal in everything we say. It's not easy, for sure, but if we focus on truth, we will love truth more and more. So focus on Jesus, who is the ultimate Truth, every day of your life (John 14:6).

. . . .

**Dear God, please help all the words of my mouth to be right
and good. Help me to always speak the truth. Help me to focus
on Jesus, who is the Truth. When I make mistakes and choose
dishonesty, please help me to admit my wrongdoing and make
it right. Thank You for Your forgiveness and grace. Amen.**

LET GOD LEAD YOU IN TRUTH

Show me Your ways, O Lord. Teach me Your paths. Lead me in Your truth and teach me. For You are the God Who saves me.

PSALM 25:4–5

Truth is so important, especially in a world where it seems harder and harder to find. Let God through His Word be your number one source of truth, and let all of these scriptures remind you how important it is:

- "The honor of good people will lead them, but those who hurt others will be destroyed by their own false ways" (Proverbs 11:3).
- "A man who tells lies about someone will be punished. He who tells lies will be lost" (Proverbs 19:9).
- "Do your best to know that God is pleased with you. Be as a workman who has nothing to be ashamed of. Teach the words of truth in the right way. Do not listen to foolish talk about things that mean nothing. It only leads people farther away from God" (2 Timothy 2:15–16).

Dear God, Your Word is the ultimate truth! Help me to grow in truth and love and wisdom and share it all with others. Amen.

DO WHAT IS RIGHT IN THE EYES OF THE LORD

*Josiah was eight years old when he became king. He ruled
for thirty-one years in Jerusalem. His mother's name was
Jedidah the daughter of Adaiah of Bozkath. Josiah did what
is right in the eyes of the Lord. He walked in all the way of his
father David. He did not turn aside to the right or to the left.*

2 KINGS 22:1–2

Can you imagine becoming queen at the age you are now, like
Josiah became king at eight years old? Wow! What would you
do in your leadership role? Hopefully you'd want to be a lot like
Josiah was. The Bible says he "did what is right in the eyes of the
Lord." That should be our goal in everything we do too, even if we
never become rulers of the land. We are always leaders to others
as long as we are following Jesus—because people who don't yet
follow Jesus look to us to lead them to His love and truth.

**Dear God, I want to be like Josiah, doing what is right
in Your eyes. I don't want to turn aside to the left or
right. I want to focus straight on You. Please help me so
that I can do Your will and lead others to You! Amen.**

JEREMIAH'S WARNINGS

"I will tell how they are to be punished for all their sin. For they have turned away from Me and have given gifts to other gods, and worshiped the works of their own hands. Now get ready. Stand up and tell them everything that I tell you. Do not be afraid of them."

JEREMIAH 1:16–17

After King Josiah died, the nation of Judah turned almost completely away from God. So God called the prophet Jeremiah to warn the people of Judah about the punishment and trouble and suffering coming their way. It helps remind us today to never choose to turn away from God and His perfect ways. He always knows and wants what is best for us!

• •

Dear God, thank You for the warnings from Jeremiah. Please help me to never turn away from worshipping and following You. Amen.

BETTER THAN HAPPINESS

*You will show me the way of life. Being with You is to be
full of joy. In Your right hand there is happiness forever.*

PSALM 16:11

Our feelings change so quickly and easily. Something that made
you happy last year or even a month ago might seem totally boring
to you now. So, real joy is always much better than happiness. Let
these scriptures help teach and guide you about knowing real joy:

- "I have placed the Lord always in front of me. Because
  He is at my right hand, I will not be moved. And so my
  heart is glad. My soul is full of joy" (Psalm 16:8–9).
- "You have never seen Him but you love Him. You cannot
  see Him now but you are putting your trust in Him. And
  you have joy so great that words cannot tell about it.
  You will get what your faith is looking for, which is to be
  saved from the punishment of sin" (1 Peter 1:8–9).
- "The joy of the Lord is your strength" (Nehemiah 8:10).

**Dear God, help me to remember that feelings
and happiness change, but my real and true
and constant joy is always in You! Amen.**

DON'T BE LIKE THE ONES WHO DO WRONG

Do not want to be like those who do wrong. . . . Trust in the Lord, and do good. . . . Be happy in the Lord. And He will give you the desires of your heart. Give your way over to the Lord. Trust in Him also. And He will do it. He will make your being right and good show as the light, and your wise actions as the noon day. Rest in the Lord and be willing to wait for Him. Do not trouble yourself when all goes well with the one who carries out his sinful plans. . . . For those who do wrong will be cut off. But those who wait for the Lord will be given the earth.

PSALM 37:1, 3–7, 9

Sometimes it seems like the very ones who do wrong are the ones who have everything going right for them. It's so frustrating! But it's not true. Everything is not going right for them if they are not trusting in God and letting Him lead. Do your best to ignore those who do wrong. Stay far away from their sin and their plans. Follow God's plans, and wait for Him to bless you instead.

· ·

Dear God, help me not to want to be like those who do wrong. Help me to focus on loving and obeying You. I trust You to bless me. Amen.

YOU'RE BETTER THAN THE BIRDS

"Do not worry about your life. Do not worry about what you are going to eat and drink. Do not worry about what you are going to wear. Is not life more important than food? Is not the body more important than clothes? Look at the birds in the sky. They do not plant seeds. They do not gather grain. They do not put grain into a building to keep. Yet your Father in heaven feeds them! Are you not more important than the birds?"
MATTHEW 6:25–26

Birds love to fly and find their food and build their nests. They know how to live their cute little bird lives because God takes care of them. Jesus wants you to remember that you're much more important than any bird. If we worry about having enough food to eat or clothes to wear, we're forgetting that God takes care of everything in His creation, and people are the best part of His creation. We only need to trust Him, and He will make sure we have everything we need.

• •

Dear God, remind me with every little bird I see that You will always take good care of me. Amen.

THE LORD IS YOUR SHEPHERD

The Lord is my Shepherd. I will have everything I need. He lets me rest in fields of green grass. He leads me beside the quiet waters. He makes me strong again. He leads me in the way of living right with Himself which brings honor to His name. Yes, even if I walk through the valley of the shadow of death, I will not be afraid of anything, because You are with me. You have a walking stick with which to guide and one with which to help. These comfort me. You are making a table of food ready for me in front of those who hate me. You have poured oil on my head. I have everything I need. For sure, You will give me goodness and loving-kindness all the days of my life. Then I will live with You in Your house forever.

PSALM 23

This is one of the most famous passages of the Bible. Do you see why? It gives strength and courage and peace, in good times and bad. It's so good to read and remember the truth that God leads you and cares for you like a Good Shepherd here on earth—until the day you're with Him forever in heaven.

• •

Dear Lord, thank You for all the ways You love and care for me. Thank You for being my Good Shepherd. Amen.

PETER'S BIG MISTAKE

Peter said to Jesus, "Even if all men give up and turn away because of You, I will never." Jesus said to him, "For sure, I tell you, before a rooster crows this night, you will say three times you do not know Me." Peter said to Him, "Even if I have to die with You, I will never say I do not know You."

MATTHEW 26:33–35

Jesus' close friend Peter made a promise to Jesus that there was no way he would ever deny knowing Jesus. It was unthinkable to Peter. But then when Jesus was captured and taken to be killed, Peter felt scared and forgot his promise. He did deny Jesus exactly like Jesus had warned. Afterward, Peter felt so sad and ashamed of himself (Matthew 26:69–75). Still, Jesus loved and forgave Peter, and Peter went on to do great things to spread the news of Jesus. Jesus loves and forgives us. He doesn't want to hold our sins against us. He wants us to continue to share His Good News.

• •

Dear Jesus, when I mess up, help me remember how Peter messed up. You love and forgive, and I will continue to live for You and share Your Good News. Amen.

PERFECT PRAYER

He took Peter and the two sons of Zebedee with Him.
He began to have much sorrow and a heavy heart.
Then He said to them, "My soul is very sad. My soul is
so full of sorrow I am ready to die. You stay here and
watch with Me." He went on a little farther and got
down with His face on the ground. He prayed, "My
Father, if it can be done, take away what is before
Me. Even so, not what I want but what You want."
MATTHEW 26:37–39

Jesus gave us the perfect example of prayer, both when He taught us to pray (Matthew 6:9–13) and when He prayed before he was killed on the cross. He knew what an awful thing was about to happen to Him, and He was honest that He didn't want to do it. But still He prayed, "Not what I want but what You want." He knew His Father's way was best, even if it would be horribly hard at first.

● ●

Dear Jesus, thank You for going through such an awful death to save me from my sin. I'm so sorry and so grateful. But I'm so glad You rose to life again! And I'm so glad for Your examples of prayer. Help me to pray not for what I want but what God wants, like You did. Amen.

JESUS LOVES TO SAVE

Those who walked by shook their heads and laughed at Him. They said, "You are the One Who could destroy the house of God and build it up again in three days. Now save Yourself. If You are the Son of God, come down from the cross." . . . And the robbers who were nailed to crosses beside Him made fun of Him the same way also.
MATTHEW 27:39–40, 44

The two robbers who were killed on crosses at the same time as Jesus both made fun of Jesus, according to the book of Matthew. But in the book of Luke (23:39–43) we read that one of the robbers must have changed his mind. He admitted his own sins and knew that Jesus had done nothing wrong. He chose to believe in Jesus and asked Jesus to bring him to heaven. And Jesus promised that the man would soon be in paradise with Him. Jesus wants all people to repent of sin and believe in Him up until their very last second of life here on earth. Jesus loves and wants to save everyone.

• •

Dear Jesus, thank You for Your love for all people and how You want to save anyone and everyone. Help me to help others admit their sin and believe in You as our only Savior. Amen.

HE IS ALIVE!

The angel said to the women, "Do not be afraid. I know you are looking for Jesus Who was nailed to the cross. He is not here! He has risen from the dead as He said He would. Come and see the place where the Lord lay. Run fast and tell His followers that He is risen from the dead. He is going before you to the country of Galilee. You will see Him there as I have told you." They went away from the grave in a hurry. They were afraid and yet had much joy. They ran to tell the news to His followers. As they went to tell the followers, Jesus met them and said hello to them. They came and held His feet and worshiped Him.

MATTHEW 28:5–9

Can you imagine being one of these women, these dear friends of Jesus? It had to be the best surprise ever to hear the angel's news and then meet up with Jesus who was not dead but alive again! That powerful news is what we still trust today. Jesus is not dead. He is alive!

• •

Dear Jesus, I believe You died to save me from my sin, but You did not stay dead. You are alive! You are my hope and the hope of the whole world. Amen.

MAKE EACH OTHER STRONGER

First of all, I keep thanking my God, through Jesus Christ, for all of you. This is because the whole world knows of your faith in Christ. God knows how I work for Him. He knows how I preach with all my heart the Good News about His Son. He knows how I always pray for you. I pray that I might be able to visit you, if God wants me to. I want to see you so I can share some special gift of the Holy Spirit with you. It will make you strong. Both of us need help. I can help make your faith strong and you can do the same for me. We need each other.

<small>ROMANS 1:8–12</small>

Do you feel grateful for your family and friends who also follow Jesus and aren't afraid to show it? You totally should! We all need one another, and together we are stronger. We encourage one another by sharing the gifts we've received from the Holy Spirit, by telling how God is working in our lives, and by reminding one another of the truths of the Bible.

• •

Dear God, thank You for the family and friends in my life who help make my faith in You stronger and stronger. Help me to encourage and make them stronger too. Amen.

PERFECT PEACE

*"Peace I leave with you. My peace I give to you.
I do not give peace to you as the world gives.
Do not let your hearts be troubled or afraid."*

JOHN 14:27

Jesus said these words to His disciples, and they are for you today too. You have supernatural peace given to you by Jesus. Peaceful things here on earth—a relaxing beach, a quiet afternoon, a nice time with family and friends—sure are nice, but they are not the deep, constant, miraculous peace that only Jesus can give. Whenever you feel troubled or afraid, let the Holy Spirit help you remember the perfect peace of Jesus.

• •

Dear Jesus, anytime I am troubled or afraid, please calm me down and quiet my mind and heart through Your Holy Spirit in me. Always remind me of Your perfect peace. Amen.

LOVES COMES FROM GOD

Dear friends, let us love each other, because love comes from God. Those who love are God's children and they know God. Those who do not love do not know God because God is love. God has shown His love to us by sending His only Son into the world. God did this so we might have life through Christ. This is love!

1 JOHN 4:7–10

When you know someone loves you, it gives you courage and so much more, doesn't it? You know that whatever hard things happen, you have someone to give you a hug, to encourage you, to remind you of all the good things in life and all the ways you are blessed and cared for. If you have even just one person loving you, supporting you, comforting you, and cheering you on, you have so much more courage and strength and confidence. All of that ultimately comes from God. He is love itself, and He is the source of every good and perfect love.

- -

Dear God, thank You for showing us what love is and letting people love one another in good and perfect ways that give us courage and so much more. Amen.

THERE'S NO POWER IN WORRY

Do not worry. Learn to pray about everything. Give thanks to God as you ask Him for what you need. The peace of God is much greater than the human mind can understand. This peace will keep your hearts and minds through Christ Jesus.

PHILIPPIANS 4:6–7

There is no power in worry; it will only make you weak. But there is power in prayer. As you pray and ask God for what you need, don't forget to focus on your blessings. When you think of the bazillion ways God has already blessed you and provided for you, you'll realize there is nothing to worry about. Just like He has in the past, God will always continue to bless you and provide for you. Thank Him and praise Him for who He is and all He has done. Then let His amazing peace fill you up and chase away whatever worries you might have.

• •

Dear God, help me to remember there is no power in worry, but there is power in prayer! Thank You for all the ways You have blessed and helped me and for all the ways You will continue to. Amen.

JUST SAY THE WORD

A captain of the army came to Him. He asked for help, saying, "Lord, my servant is sick in bed. He is not able to move his body. He is in much pain." Jesus said to the captain, "I will come and heal him." The captain said, "Lord, I am not good enough for You to come to my house. Only speak the word, and my servant will be healed". . . . When Jesus heard this, He was surprised and wondered about it. He said to those who followed Him, "For sure, I tell you, I have not found so much faith in the Jewish nation. . . ." Jesus said to the captain, "Go your way. It is done for you even as you had faith to believe." The servant was healed at that time.

MATTHEW 8:5–10, 13

We need to always have faith like this army captain. Jesus offered to come to his house to heal his servant, but the captain knew Jesus could just say the word from anywhere and the servant would be healed. The captain fully believed in Jesus' awesome power, and so should we!

• •

Dear Jesus, just say the word and You can do anything! I believe in Your great power. Amen.

ALWAYS IN FRONT OF YOU

I will give honor and thanks to the Lord, Who has told me what to do. Yes, even at night my mind teaches me. I have placed the Lord always in front of me. Because He is at my right hand, I will not be moved. And so my heart is glad. My soul is full of joy. My body also will rest without fear. For You will not give me over to the grave. And You will not allow Your Holy One to return to dust.

PSALM 16:7–10

Can you truly say, like the writer of this psalm, that you always put the Lord in front of you? Why is that a good idea? It's a good idea because it means you're letting God lead you. And when you do, you will be steady and stable in all your life—even when hard times come. No matter what comes your way, God will give you joy and peace and rest without fear.

. . . .

Dear God, I want to honestly be able to say that I always put You in front of me. I don't want to be the leader of my life. I know You will lead me best, and I want to follow You! Amen.

GET BACK TO WORK

*" 'Be strong, all you people of the land,' says the
Lord. 'Do the work, for I am with you,' says the Lord
of All. 'As I promised you when you came out of
Egypt, My Spirit is with you. Do not be afraid.' "*

HAGGAI 2:4–5

At first God's people had a good plan and a good start on the
work of rebuilding the temple in Jerusalem, but then they got
distracted. We know what that's like. Sometimes we get excited
about good things God has asked us to do, and we enjoy them for
a while, but then we get off track and start doing our own thing
instead. The prophet Haggai had a message back then that is
for us today too: get back to work! God's spirit is with us, and He
wants to help us do the things He has asked us to do.

• •

**Dear God, please forgive me when I get off track from
the good work You've given me to do. I want to get
back to work. Please show me and lead me. Amen.**

LET HIM MAKE YOU STRONG

It is good to hear that your faith is so strong in Christ. As you have put your trust in Christ Jesus the Lord to save you from the punishment of sin, now let Him lead you in every step. Have your roots planted deep in Christ. Grow in Him. Get your strength from Him. Let Him make you strong in the faith as you have been taught. Your life should be full of thanks to Him.

COLOSSIANS 2:5–7

How strong would you say your faith is in Christ? Can it always get stronger? It sure can! As you let Him lead you in every step through the Holy Spirit, your roots will grow deeper and deeper into Him. The deeper the roots of a tree go, the stronger it is. The deeper its roots grow, the harder it is for the tree to fall. The same goes for you. The deeper your roots grow in Jesus, the stronger you are in your faith, and the harder it is for any hard thing in life to make you fall.

• •

Dear Jesus, please keep me growing deeper roots into You with stronger faith each day as You lead me in every step. Amen.

NOTHING CAN KEEP GOD'S LOVE AWAY

We have power over all these things through Jesus Who loves us so much. For I know that nothing can keep us from the love of God. Death cannot! Life cannot! Angels cannot! Leaders cannot! Any other power cannot! Hard things now or in the future cannot! The world above or the world below cannot! Any other living thing cannot keep us away from the love of God which is ours through Christ Jesus our Lord.

ROMANS 8:37–39

God's Word promises that we have great power through Jesus who loves us so much. And absolutely nothing, not one single thing, can ever keep God's love away from us. So remember that anything you might feel afraid of today cannot defeat you because God's love never leaves you.

- -

Dear God, don't let me forget the power of Your love that never, ever leaves me. There is nothing and no one more loving and powerful than You! I'm so grateful You are my Lord and Savior. I'm so grateful for Your Holy Spirit living in me. Amen.

FORGIVE AND BE FORGIVEN

"If you forgive people their sins, your Father in heaven will forgive your sins also. If you do not forgive people their sins, your Father will not forgive your sins."

MATTHEW 6:14–15

Has someone hurt you or teased you or made you mad recently? How did you feel about forgiving that person? It's not always easy. But the Bible is clear that our willingness to forgive is a big deal. Jesus said that God won't forgive our sins if we don't forgive others. And yikes, we sure do need Him to forgive our mistakes! When we are upset with someone who treated us badly, we have to think of how much we need forgiveness for the things we do wrong too. Jesus forgives so generously because He died on the cross to forgive our sins, so we should want to give forgiveness generously as well.

- -

Dear Jesus, when it's hard to forgive, help me to think about how thankful I am that You forgive my sins. I want to be like You. Amen.

COURAGE IN SADNESS

My eyes become weak from crying. My spirit is very troubled. My heart is poured out in sorrow, because my people have been destroyed.
LAMENTATIONS 2:11

Sometimes it's courageous to admit how sad we are. In the book of Lamentations, Jeremiah wrote down all of his sadness about the way the city of Jerusalem had been destroyed because the people turned away from God. The word *lamentation* means an expression of sorrow. Sometimes when you feel sad about something, it can be helpful to write down your sad feelings as you tell God about them and let Him comfort you and strengthen you again. Share them with trusted loved ones too because God will use their care to help you.

• •

Dear God, help me to remember it's okay to be sad. Help me to share all my feelings with You and with people who love me. I trust You will bring me the comfort and encouragement I need. Amen.

BECAUSE OF THE POWER OF GOD

*When I was with you, I was weak. I was afraid and
I shook. What I had to say when I preached was not in
big sounding words of man's wisdom. But it was given
in the power of the Holy Spirit. In this way, you do not
have faith in Christ because of the wisdom of men.
You have faith in Christ because of the power of God.*

1 CORINTHIANS 2:3–5

Do you ever feel afraid to share your faith like the apostle Paul described in this scripture? Then let Paul encourage you. He didn't feel like he had all the best-sounding words that would make everyone want to listen to him either. Paul just knew about Jesus; Paul knew Jesus had transformed his life, and Paul knew that Jesus died on the cross and rose again to save people from their sin and give them eternal life. It is the power of God working in you through His Holy Spirit that helps you share the Good News of Jesus. All you have to do is let God work.

**Dear God, it's all You! Please just use me as You want,
with Your words and wisdom, Your truth and power, to
help others know You and trust Jesus as Savior. Amen.**

LEARN FROM EZEKIEL

" 'As I live,' says the Lord God, 'I am not pleased when sinful people die. But I am pleased when the sinful turn from their way and live. Turn! Turn from your sinful ways!' "

EZEKIEL 33:11

Ezekiel was God's prophet whose name means "strengthened by God." He sure needed extra strength because sometimes God told Ezekiel to do some pretty weird-sounding things. For example, Ezekiel was told to lie on his left side for 390 days to show the nation of Israel it would be punished for 390 years for turning away from God. But like Ezekiel 33:11 tells us, God is never happy when people are punished for their sins. He wants people to turn away from sin and let Him give them the best kind of life by following Him.

• •

Dear God, thank You for how much You want people to turn away from sin. Help me to help people realize how much You love us. Amen.

HOLD ON TO HIM

"A man who tells what is going to happen or a dreamer of dreams may come among you. . . . But if he says to you, 'Let us follow other gods (whom you have not known) and let us worship them,' do not listen to the words of that man who tells you what will happen or that dreamer of dreams. For the Lord your God is putting you to the test to see if you love the Lord your God with all your heart and with all your soul. Follow the Lord your God and fear Him. Keep His Laws, and listen to His voice. Work for Him, and hold on to Him."

DEUTERONOMY 13:1–4

God will allow tests in your life to see if your faith in the one true God is real and if you love Him with all your heart and soul. These are tests you sure do want to get an A+ on! So follow God, obey Him, work for Him, listen to Him. Hold on tight to the one real God, the only One worthy of always holding on to.

• •

Dear God, please help me to pass the tests of showing You how much I love You and believe in You. I never want to stop holding on to You and You alone. Amen.

YOU KNOW THE HOLY WRITINGS PART 1

Hold on to what you have learned and know to be true. Remember where you learned them. You have known the Holy Writings since you were a child. They are able to give you wisdom that leads to being saved from the punishment of sin by putting your trust in Christ Jesus.

2 TIMOTHY 3:14–15

If you're reading this book that is full of scripture from God's Word, and if you're learning God's Word in other ways (like at church and with your family and simply opening up your Bible to read it regularly), then exactly like this verse says, "you have known the Holy Writings since you were a child." The Bible gives you the wisdom you need throughout your life. It encourages you to make good choices and trust Jesus with everything! What a wonderful way to live!

• •

Dear God, thank You for the blessing of teaching me from Your Holy Writings even now while I'm a kid. Not everyone has that blessing as a kid. Help me now and as I grow to continue to love and learn from Your Word and to help others love it and learn from it too. Amen.

YOU KNOW THE HOLY WRITINGS PART 2

All the Holy Writings are God-given and are made alive by Him. Man is helped when he is taught God's Word. It shows what is wrong. It changes the way of a man's life. It shows him how to be right with God. It gives the man who belongs to God everything he needs to work well for Him.
2 TIMOTHY 3:16–17

You can have total trust in God's Word because it wasn't just written by people but by God Himself working through the authors of the Bible. God made His Word alive back in ancient times, and it is still alive today. All the Holy Writings guide us to show us what is wrong in our lives and to change us and help us live right with God and do His will.

• •

Dear God, help me not to forget the living power of Your Word. It's sure not just an ordinary book—it is the most incredible book ever, the one You use to speak to all people and help us in this life. I know that, ultimately, its guidance will lead to forever life with You! Amen.

RICH IN EVERY WAY

He has made your lives rich in every way. Now you have power to speak for Him. He gave you good understanding. This shows that what I told you about Christ and what He could do for you has been done in your lives. You have the gifts of the Holy Spirit that you need while you wait for the Lord Jesus Christ to come again. Christ will keep you strong until He comes again.

1 CORINTHIANS 1:5–8

Think about all the ways God has made your life "rich in every way." Do you have or can you start a gratitude journal to list them and focus on them? When you thank and praise God often for all His goodness to you, it's hard to be worried or scared about anything. Ask God to constantly show you the gifts of the Holy Spirit that He has given. Let Him tell you how He wants you to use them specifically in this world until He comes again. Jesus knows you and loves you and will keep you strong until the day of His return!

• •

Dear God, thank You for making me rich in every way. Thank You for Your power in me. Thank You for giving me good understanding. Please keep me strong and help me to use the gifts You have given me in the ways You want me to. Amen.

FAITH-FULL FRIENDS

Some men took a man who was not able to move his body to Jesus. He was carried on a bed. They looked for a way to take the man into the house where Jesus was. But they could not find a way to take him in because of so many people. They made a hole in the roof over where Jesus stood. Then they let the bed with the sick man on it down before Jesus. When Jesus saw their faith, He said to the man, "Friend, your sins are forgiven."
LUKE 5:18–20

Wow, this man who was paralyzed, totally unable to move, sure had good friends. They had faith that Jesus could heal him, and they were willing to do whatever it took to get their friend to Jesus, even if it meant making a hole in the roof above Jesus and lowering their friend down through the hole to gently land right in front of Him. This didn't upset Jesus at all. Clearly it made Him happy that these friends had such great faith in Him!

• •

Dear God, please bless me with friends who are so full of faith in You that they are willing to do whatever it takes to help others know You and Your power. Thank You for Your awesome power to heal and to save all people who believe in You. Amen.

COURAGEOUS AND GENEROUS

"Give, and it will be given to you. You will have more than enough. It can be pushed down and shaken together and it will still run over as it is given to you. The way you give to others is the way you will receive in return."

LUKE 6:38

It takes courage to be generous. You have to be brave to give away what you have to others because you have to trust that you will still have what you need. No worries! God will always give you enough for your own needs as you help provide for the needs of others. The Bible promises it. The more you give, God will give you even more. He loves to reward you when you share the gifts that ultimately always come from Him.

• •

Dear God, please help me always be able to happily give to others. I don't ever want to be afraid of not having enough for myself. I trust that You will always provide for and bless me. Amen.

REMEMBER ZACCHEUS

Zaccheus wanted to see Jesus but he could not because so many people were there and he was a short man. He ran ahead and got up into a sycamore tree to see Him. Jesus was going by that way.

LUKE 19:3–4

It's fun to think about how Zaccheus climbed a tree to see Jesus because he was too short to see above the crowd. The move was clever of him and showed how much he was interested in Jesus. Zaccheus had been a cheater with money, taking from others to make himself rich. But a relationship with Jesus changed his life and made him want to make things right where he had sinned against others. Let the story of Zaccheus remind you to always be interested in Jesus too. Even more important, let it remind you how the power of Jesus in someone's life can totally transform that person from bad to good.

Dear Jesus, please do Your good work of transforming people from bad to good. Help more and more people to want to know You as Savior, and use me however You want to share Your power, truth, and love. Amen.

PROTECTED AND READY TO FIGHT

Be strong with the Lord's strength. Put on the things God gives you to fight with. Then you will not fall into the traps of the devil. . . . Wear a belt of truth around your body. Wear a piece of iron over your chest which is being right with God. Wear shoes on your feet which are the Good News of peace. Most important of all, you need a covering of faith in front of you. This is to put out the fire-arrows of the devil. The covering for your head is that you have been saved from the punishment of sin. Take the sword of the Spirit which is the Word of God.

EPHESIANS 6:10–11, 14–17

God knows we will have battles in this world—battles with our enemy the devil and the evil spirits of darkness in the world. So He gave us armor and weapons to be protected and ready to fight! Think about these verses when you feel under attack, and remember that God will never let the devil defeat you.

• •

Dear God, thank You for protecting me and equipping me in every battle against evil. I am strong and fierce and able to fight because of You. Amen.

WATCH OUT FOR THE WOLVES

"Watch out for false teachers. They come to you dressed as if they were sheep. On the inside they are hungry wolves. You will know them by their fruit. Do men pick grapes from thorns? Do men pick figs from thistles? It is true, every good tree has good fruit. Every bad tree has bad fruit. A good tree cannot have bad fruit. A bad tree cannot have good fruit. Every tree that does not have good fruit is cut down and thrown into the fire. So you will know them by their fruit."

MATTHEW 7:15–20

Sheep and wolves and fruit? What does all this mean? It means to watch out for false teachers—people who say they love God and His Word but are sneaky. These people actually try to lead others away from knowing Jesus as their Savior. We will know them by the fruit in their lives, which means the things they've done or not done. We need so much wisdom from God to be able to spot false teachers, who are like wolves, and stay away from them.

• •

Dear God, please give me wisdom and show me who the sneaky wolves are so I can avoid them. Amen.

KNOWING WHO YOU ARE

And God made man in His own likeness. In the likeness
of God He made him. He made both male and female.
GENESIS 1:27

More and more people these days sadly seem to be lost, trying to find their identities. But all they need to do is look to God! His Word is clear in Genesis 1 that God made people in His likeness. He has made boys and girls to grow up into men and women, and He has given us the Bible to guide us in how to live and love like He does. When people choose to accept Jesus as Savior, they become new creations. They can say, "Christ lives in me. The life I now live in this body, I live by putting my trust in the Son of God. He was the One Who loved me and gave Himself for me" (Galatians 2:20).

• •

Dear God, I'm so thankful that I can say, "Christ lives in me!" I know who I am. I am Your child, and I live my life for Jesus. Amen.

IMAGINE THE BEST, NOT THE WORST

God is our safe place and our strength. He is always our help when we are in trouble. So we will not be afraid, even if the earth is shaken and the mountains fall into the center of the sea, and even if its waters go wild with storm and the mountains shake with its action.

PSALM 46:1–3

Sometimes we get scared and worry because we imagine the worst that can happen and then we focus on that. So we need this scripture to remind us that there is no horrible thing we can think of that God cannot help us with. He is always our Help when we are in trouble, no matter how awful the trouble is. Instead of imagining the worst, we should always think of the best—that God is our Safe Place and our Strength!

• •

Dear God, thank You that You will always be my Help. You save and protect me from even the worst kind of trouble. Amen.

WHO'S THE BOSS?

If your sinful old self is the boss over your mind, it leads to death. But if the Holy Spirit is the boss over your mind, it leads to life and peace. The mind that thinks only of ways to please the sinful old self is fighting against God. It is not able to obey God's Laws. It never can. Those who do what their sinful old selves want to do cannot please God. But you are not doing what your sinful old selves want you to do. You are doing what the Holy Spirit tells you to do, if you have God's Spirit living in you.

ROMANS 8:6–9

You might feel like your mom and dad and teachers and coaches and leaders are all the boss of you right now and you just can't wait to be your own boss someday. But guess what? It's a bad idea to want to be your own boss! The Bible says if your sinful self is your boss, it will lead to death. But if God's Holy Spirit is your boss, that will lead to life and peace. He wants to boss you in the best kind of ways to lead you to the very best blessings.

• •

Dear God, please help me not to want to be my own boss but to let Your Holy Spirit guide and direct me in everything I do. Amen.

MAYBE AN ANGEL?

*"Last night an angel of God stood by
me and said, 'Do not be afraid, Paul.'"*

ACTS 27:23–24

Have you ever had a stranger say something to you that was exactly what you needed to hear? Maybe you were sad and someone comforted you. Maybe you were scared and someone reassured and encouraged you. What if that someone was really an angel sent by God? This could totally be true, especially if you'd never seen the person before and haven't ever again! Whenever you have an experience like that, notice and thank God for it. Whether it was an angel or not, God used that someone in your life to help you, and you can trust that He will always send the right people and/or angels to you when you need them.

• •

**Dear God, thank You for the times You have used people I
don't even know to help me and encourage me. It's cool to
think they might have been angels! Maybe they were and
maybe they weren't, but I never want to forget how You help
me through all kinds of people and in all kinds of ways. Amen.**

WE ARE CHILDREN OF GOD

All those who are led by the Holy Spirit are sons of God. You should not act like people who are owned by someone. They are always afraid. Instead, the Holy Spirit makes us His sons, and we can call to Him, "My Father." For the Holy Spirit speaks to us and tells our spirit that we are children of God. If we are children of God, we will receive everything He has promised us. We will share with Christ all the things God has given to Him.

ROMANS 8:14–17

You are true royalty as a daughter of the one true King, dear girl, and you will inherit a royal eternal kingdom in perfect paradise one day! This scripture assures you that you are a child of God, led by the Holy Spirit. You never need to be afraid of anything because the almighty King of all kings is your Father. You can have all courage and all confidence when you focus on the promises of God, trusting that one day you will share all the greatness of Jesus Christ.

• •

Dear God, You are my King and You are my dear Father. I am so grateful to be Your child. Please keep me focused on Your promises, and give me all courage and confidence, all the time. Amen.

WHEN WE WONDER WHY

I am sure that our suffering now cannot be compared to the shining-greatness that He is going to give us. Everything that has been made in the world is waiting for the day when God will make His sons known. Everything that has been made in the world is weak. It is not that the world wanted it to be that way. God allowed it to be that way. Yet there is hope. Everything that has been made in the world will be set free from the power that can destroy.

ROMANS 8:18–21

Sometimes when we're begging God for help and an answer, He does not just suddenly fix things like we want. We sure wish He would—so when He doesn't, our trust in Him can really be shaken as we wonder why. But we have to stand strong and keep on trusting. We have to look for the ways God is answering our prayers, even when we don't see the exact answer we're hoping for.

• •

Dear God, please help me to keep trusting You even when I'm confused about why You don't fix things how I want You to. Please hold me tight when I'm hurting. I know You love me. Amen.

GOD KNOWS IT ALL

O Lord, You have looked through me and have known me. You know when I sit down and when I get up. You understand my thoughts from far away. You look over my path and my lying down. You know all my ways very well. Even before I speak a word, O Lord, You know it all. You have closed me in from behind and in front. And You have laid Your hand upon me. All You know is too great for me. It is too much for me to understand. Where can I go from Your Spirit? Or where can I run away from where You are?

PSALM 139:1–7

God knows absolutely everything about you—every move, every word, every choice, every thought. That's nothing to worry about if you love God and are letting the Holy Spirit lead your life. Let it comfort you to know that God sees and knows all. Because He does, He can care for you, protect you, teach you, and love you like no one else possibly can.

• •

Dear God, it's crazy amazing to think about how You know everything—including every single thing about me. And You love me and care for me and lead me through it all. Thank You! Amen.

HOW TO SHINE

God is helping you obey Him. God is doing what He wants done in you. Be glad you can do the things you should be doing. Do all things without arguing and talking about how you wish you did not have to do them. In that way, you can prove yourselves to be without blame. You are God's children and no one can talk against you, even in a sin-loving and sin-sick world. You are to shine as lights among the sinful people of this world.
PHILIPPIANS 2:13–15

It's hard not to grumble and complain sometimes, right? What ways do you struggle with that the most? With homework? With chores? With helping out your siblings? But don't forget that in all these things God is doing what He wants done in you. As you do any and every task, remember that the Holy Spirit is in you, and let Him help you do it with purpose and love and joy. That's how you shine your light!

• •

Dear God, do what You want done in my life. Help me to do all the things You've given me to do with a good attitude. Help me to shine my light with love and joy to point others to You! Amen.

JESUS MAKES US CLEAN

The blood of Jesus Christ, His Son, makes our lives clean from all sin. If we say that we have no sin, we lie to ourselves and the truth is not in us. If we tell Him our sins, He is faithful and we can depend on Him to forgive us of our sins. He will make our lives clean from all sin.

1 JOHN 1:7–9

Sin is dark and dirty, like after playing in the mud! But through Jesus we are made clean from the bad choices and mistakes we make. It's sad when people won't simply admit that they make mistakes and are sinners in need of a Savior. We need to share the truth of that with everyone we can. No, we shouldn't be proud of our sins, but we should be proud of and grateful for the One who can wash them away.

• •

Dear Jesus, I know I'm a sinner, but thank You for making me clean. Thank You for letting me live in God's light because You take my sin away. Help me to show others how wonderful this is. Amen.

GOD'S HAND WILL HELP YOU

Even if I walk into trouble, You will keep my life safe. You will put out Your hand against the anger of those who hate me. And Your right hand will save me. The Lord will finish the work He started for me. O Lord, Your loving-kindness lasts forever.

PSALM 138:7–8

Have you ever felt like someone truly hates you? Maybe a bully or mean girl at school is making your life miserable. If that's the case, remember and pray this scripture. God can put out His hand to protect you against any anger of anyone who might treat you hatefully. Pray to ask Him to do so, and then thank and praise Him when He does.

• •

Dear God, I feel hated by some people right now, and I'm overwhelmed. Please put out Your hand against them to protect and save me. Show me Your love and kindness, and help me to do the good works You have planned for me. Amen.

GOD'S GREAT BIG LOVE

I pray that Christ may live in your hearts by faith. I pray that you will be filled with love. I pray that you will be able to understand how wide and how long and how high and how deep His love is. I pray that you will know the love of Christ. His love goes beyond anything we can understand. I pray that you will be filled with God Himself. God is able to do much more than we ask or think through His power working in us.

EPHESIANS 3:17–20

This is a powerful prayer from Paul in the Bible, one that we need to pray for ourselves and for others all the time today too. If we could really, fully understand how *big* God's love is for us, we would never worry or be scared about a thing.

• •

Dear God, please help me to learn more and more about Your love, especially through Your Word and by noticing all the ways You are blessing me in my life. Help me to focus so much on Your great big love that my mind doesn't have any room for worry or fear. Amen.

JUST THE RIGHT WORDS

"Look out for men. They will take you up to their courts and they will hurt you in their places of worship. They will take you in front of the leaders of the people and of the kings because of Me. You will tell them and the people who do not know God about Me. When you are put into their hands, do not worry what you will say or how you will say it. The words will be given you when the time comes. It will not be you who will speak the words. The Spirit of your Father will speak through you."

MATTHEW 10:17–20

Jesus was telling His disciples that they would go out into dangerous situations, where people would hate them because they were His followers. Bad people would not want them to share the Good News about Jesus. But Jesus encouraged His friends not to worry about what others would say. The disciples would have exactly the right words because the Spirit of God would speak through them. How cool is that? The Spirit of God can speak through you too!

- -

Dear God, use me as You want to. Speak through me as You want to. Help me to share Your truth and love wherever and whenever You want. Amen.

TREASURE FOREVER

"Do not gather together for yourself riches of this earth. They will be eaten by bugs and become rusted. Men can break in and steal them. Gather together riches in heaven where they will not be eaten by bugs or become rusted. Men cannot break in and steal them. For wherever your riches are, your heart will be there also."

MATTHEW 6:19–21

Sometimes we get anxious and scared here on earth because we worry too much about what will happen to our stuff, like our money and our toys and our homes, if we don't save and protect them and find ways to get more. But this scripture helps us remember that everything of this earth can wear out or get ruined or stolen, so it's not wise to focus too much on it all anyway. We should really be focused on saving up treasure in heaven that will last forever. We do that by following God's good plans for us and loving and serving others.

• •

Dear God, please help me not to worry much over the stuff of this world. Remind me that it won't last anyway. I want to store up perfect treasure in heaven forever because I love and obey You! Amen.

PROVED BY A POWERFUL ACT

*This letter is from Paul. I am a servant owned by Jesus Christ
and a missionary chosen by God to preach His Good News. . . .
The Holy Spirit proved by a powerful act that Jesus our
Lord is the Son of God because He was raised from the
dead. Jesus has given us His loving-favor and has made
us His missionaries. We are to preach to the people of all
nations that they should obey Him and put their trust in
Him. You have been chosen to belong to Jesus Christ also.*

ROMANS 1:1–6

Paul started out the book of Romans by stating clearly that Jesus
is the Son of God and people everywhere should put their trust in
Him. The Holy Spirit proved "by a powerful act" that Jesus is truly
the Son of God by the way Jesus died but rose again. This is why
we know today that following Jesus Christ is the one true way to
know God and have eternal life. No other religion promises what
Jesus promises, with the proof He gave of rising from the dead.

• •

**Dear God, thank You that I have been chosen to belong to
Jesus! Help me, like Paul, to want to share Your Good News
so that more people will obey and trust in You! Amen.**

PIECES OF WOOD?

"How can you say to your brother, 'Let me take that small piece of wood out of your eye,' when you do not see the big piece of wood in your own eye? You pretend to be someone you are not. First, take the big piece of wood out of your own eye. Then you can see better to take the small piece of wood out of your brother's eye."

LUKE 6:41–42

Are these verses really about picking pieces of wood out of eyeballs? Yes and no. Jesus was giving an example to teach a lesson that we shouldn't be trying to show other people their problems and sins without first making sure we are working on getting rid of our own problems and sins. We shouldn't ever be hypocrites, meaning people who pretend to do no wrong and only focus on what others do wrong. We all are sinners who sure do need Jesus' awesome love and grace.

• •

Dear Jesus, please help me to be sure I'm always wanting to get rid of my own sin by admitting it and asking for forgiveness. Then, with Your wisdom, show me how You might want me to help others get rid of sin too. Amen.

HUGS FROM JESUS

They brought little children to Jesus that He might put His hand on them. The followers spoke sharp words to those who brought them. Jesus saw this and was angry with the followers. He said, "Let the little children come to Me. Do not stop them. The holy nation of God is made up of ones like these. For sure, I tell you, whoever does not receive the holy nation of God as a little child does not go into it." He took the children in His arms. He put His hands on them and prayed that good would come to them.

MARK 10:13–16

If you're ever feeling unimportant because you're a kid, read and remember this scripture. Jesus valued children so much, and He values *you* today too! He loves and treasures you. He is proud of your faith. The strong faith that kids like you have is the kind of strong faith that every grown-up needs too. In the times when you might be feeling like you don't matter, picture Jesus pulling you into a great big bear hug and reassuring you that you do. He adores you and wants what is best for you.

• •

**Dear Jesus, thank You for making me feel so loved
and important. I'm grateful for my faith in You.
Please grow it stronger every day. Amen.**

THE POWER IS YOURS

*Now, because of this, those who belong to Christ will
not suffer the punishment of sin. The power of the Holy
Spirit has made me free from the power of sin and death.
This power is mine because I belong to Christ Jesus.*

ROMANS 8:1–2

We are sadly all affected by sin and death in many different, awful
ways. But these words from Paul in the book of Romans are words
you can make your own. If you belong to Jesus because you have
asked Him to be your Savior, you will not suffer the punishment of
sin. The power of the Holy Spirit in you makes you free from the
power of sin and death. Yes, our earthly bodies will have hard
times in this world, and we will die someday, but as followers of
Jesus, our souls will never die. We will gain new bodies and go on
to eternal life with Jesus in the perfect paradise of heaven.

**Dear God, thank You for the power of the Holy Spirit making
me free from the power of sin and death. That power
of the Holy Spirit is mine because I belong to Your Son,
Jesus Christ! Hallelujah, that is so awesome! Amen.**

WATCH YOUR WORDS

*Watch your talk! No bad words should be coming
from your mouth. Say what is good. Your words
should help others grow as Christians.*
EPHESIANS 4:29

Our words matter, even if we think they don't. And it's super hard for every single one of us to always say what is good. James 3:2 says, "We all make many mistakes. If anyone does not make a mistake with his tongue by saying the wrong things, he is a perfect man." In other words, it takes a totally perfect person to never, ever make a mistake with words. And there is no perfect person other than Jesus. That's why we need so much help from God through the Holy Spirit to help us with what we say. And when we mess up, which we will, we must ask for forgiveness from God and from the ones our words have hurt. Thankfully, God loves to forgive and help us, and so we should always want to forgive and help others too.

• •

**Dear God, please help me to watch my talk and say what
is good. Forgive me when I mess this up, help others to
forgive me, and help me to forgive others. Thank You for
Your love and grace. Please help us all share it. Amen.**

BE FAITHFUL IN ALL THINGS, BIG AND SMALL

"His owner said to him, 'You have done well. You are a good and faithful servant. You have been faithful over a few things. I will put many things in your care. Come and share my joy.' "

MATTHEW 25:21

Take time to read the parable of the three servants that Jesus told in Matthew 25. Then notice how the lesson is that when we are faithful in the little things, God is happy and gives us more things to take care of and be faithful with! It is a blessing to have responsibility, do good work, and do well—and then be given more responsibility and good work to do! What are the things you have responsibility for now? Do you realize that the way you do those things now affects your whole future and the good works God will give you to do?

• •

Dear God, please help me to be faithful and hardworking and see the value and joy in that. I want to please You most of all, even in things that seem small, and do all the good things You have planned for my life. Amen.

TRUST IN JESUS' PROMISES

"Do not let your heart be troubled. You have put your trust in God, put your trust in Me also. There are many rooms in My Father's house. If it were not so, I would have told you. I am going away to make a place for you. After I go and make a place for you, I will come back and take you with Me. Then you may be where I am. You know where I am going and you know how to get there." Thomas said to Jesus, "Lord, we do not know where You are going. How can we know the way to get there?" Jesus said, "I am the Way and the Truth and the Life. No one can go to the Father except by Me."

JOHN 14:1–6

No matter what goes on in our homes and in our lives on earth, we have great hope for our forever home with Jesus in heaven. He is our Way, Truth, and Life. We can always trust in His promises—now and forever!

Dear Jesus, thank You for the perfect home You are making for me in heaven. When life here feels hard, please help me to keep pressing on with joy as I trust in Your promises and the hope I have in You. Amen.

COURAGEOUS AND PERSISTENT

Jesus told them a picture-story to show that
men should always pray and not give up.

LUKE 18:1

Jesus told a story about a woman who was persistent in asking for help. The point of the parable was to tell us to be persistent too. Jesus was trying to get us to consider that if a judge in the courts who did not even respect God was finally willing to help the woman who did not give up in asking, how much more will God help His people when we are persistent in asking for His help?

• •

Dear God, thank You that I don't need to be afraid to be persistent with You. I can ask You again and again and again for what I need. I trust You to help and provide. Amen.

BE STRONG AND BRAVE AND DO IT!

David said to his son Solomon, "Be strong. Have strength of heart, and do it. Do not be afraid or troubled, for the Lord God, my God, is with you. He will not stop helping you. He will not leave you until all the work of the house of the Lord is finished."

1 CHRONICLES 28:20

When you're facing a challenge or a lot of hard work, sometimes you just need a little pep talk like Solomon got from his dad, David. Do you have family and friends who give you good pep talks? Be sure to thank them for being encouragers in your life. And sometimes you just need to remember scripture like this and let God's Word give you the exact pep talk you need.

Dear God, thank You for the people who give me good pep talks and mostly for all the pep talks I need that come from Your Word! Help me to remember them exactly when I need them. Amen.

LEARN FROM HABAKKUK

This is the special word which Habakkuk the man of God saw. O Lord, how long must I call for help before You will hear? I cry out to You, "We are being hurt!"

HABAKKUK 1:1–2

We can all relate to asking God questions. We sometimes wonder why we have to wait so long on Him or why He doesn't answer our prayers the way we want. Habakkuk was a prophet of God who had lots of questions too. We can learn from him that even though he never got the exact answers he was hoping for from God, he got answers that reminded him of God's power and goodness. Even today in our own lives, we must remember what Habakkuk learned: that God will work out His perfect plans in His perfect timing.

• •

Dear God, like Habakkuk, I want to say that even if everything seems to be going wrong and I have no answers from You about why, "yet I will have joy in the Lord. I will be glad in the God Who saves me" (Habakkuk 3:18). Amen.

WATCHING THE SKY

A cloud carried Him away so they could not see Him. They were still looking up to heaven, watching Him go. All at once two men dressed in white stood beside them. They said, "You men of the country of Galilee, why do you stand looking up into heaven? This same Jesus Who was taken from you into heaven will return in the same way you saw Him go up into heaven."

ACTS 1:9–11

After Jesus had died and rose again, He returned to earth for forty days to prove Himself alive and teach His followers more before going up to heaven in a cloud. His friends kept watching the sky, but then two angels appeared and wanted to know what they were doing. After all, Jesus will come back again someday! It was time for His followers to get busy sharing about Jesus. Do you ever wish Jesus would hurry back in the sky right now too? I do! But while we wait, we also need to keep busy sharing the Good News that Jesus died to save us from our sin, and He is alive now and will take all who trust in Him to heaven someday.

Dear Jesus, I'm watching the sky for You, but I'll also keep busy sharing Your Good News. Amen.

WHY DAVID WASN'T SCARED

*But David said to Saul, ". . .Your servant has killed
both the lion and the bear. And this Philistine who has
not gone through our religious act will be like one of
them. For he has made fun of the armies of the living
God." And David said, "The Lord Who saved me from
the foot of the lion and from the foot of the bear, will
save me from the hand of this Philistine." Saul said
to David, "Go, and may the Lord be with you."*
1 SAMUEL 17:34, 36–37

David was sure he could fight the giant Goliath. He wasn't scared.
He knew God had helped him fight lions and bears in the past, and
so God would help him fight the Philistine giant that everyone else
was afraid of. Let David's example encourage you—sometimes
you simply need to remember all the ways God has helped you
fight and win in the past, and that can give you everything you
need to let God help you win whatever battle is in front of you now.

**Dear God, when I face a battle, remind me how You have
helped and protected me in the past. I know You will keep
on helping me right now and in the future too. Amen.**

BUILT ON ROCK

"And why do you call Me, 'Lord, Lord,' but do not do what I say? Whoever comes to Me and hears and does what I say, I will show you who he is like. He is like a man who built a house. He dug deep to put the building on rock. When the water came up and the river beat against the house, the building could not be shaken because it was built on rock. But he who hears and does not do what I say, is like a man who built a house on nothing but earth. The water beat against the house. At once it fell and was destroyed."

LUKE 6:46–49

You're so much more than courageous when your life is built on the firm foundation of Jesus. When you listen to and obey Him, by reading His Word and keeping close relationship with Him through prayer and worship, it's like you're building your life on solid rock. When you experience rains and storms and the floods of life—in other words, the bad things that come your way—your life won't crumble and wash away. You will stand strong through anything because you stand on Jesus.

Dear Jesus, I want my life to be rock solid and strong because it's built on obeying You! Amen.

OBEY HIM ANYWAY

Noah did just what God told him to do.
GENESIS 6:22

We don't know a lot about what people must have thought of Noah while he was building the ark. Did they walk past his construction site and laugh at him? Did they spread mean jokes and gossip about him? Even if they did, in the end, what happened? Only Noah and his family were saved from the flood because they listened to God. Even if God asks you to do things that might seem crazy to others, even if friends laugh at you and gossip about you for following Jesus, obey Him anyway. In the end, you will see how God was working in your life in the best ways.

• •

Dear God, help me to listen and follow and obey You, even if it seems crazy at first. I trust You will help me see the good plans and happy endings You have for me. Amen.

TAKE A TIME-OUT

[Jesus] said to them, "Come away from
the people. Be by yourselves and rest."
MARK 6:31

Maybe you had time-outs when you got into trouble as a little kid. But guess what? Everyone needs time-outs sometimes—in trouble or not and at every age—even if you're an extrovert who loves to be around people as much as possible. We all must have breaks from others sometimes to just be alone and rest. In this scripture Jesus and His friends, the disciples, had been traveling and teaching so much that they were in great need of a time-out away from people, so they went off by themselves in a boat. It wasn't unkind or unloving of them, it was just necessary to relax and recharge. Don't forget that it's necessary and good for you sometimes too.

· ·

Dear God, please help me to have wisdom about taking
time-outs when I need them, to rest and recharge
and especially to listen well to You. Amen.

YOU ARE WEAK; GOD IS NOT

Christ is not weak when He works in your hearts. He uses His power in you. Christ's weak human body died on a cross. It is by God's power that Christ lives today. We are weak. We are as He was. But we will be alive with Christ through the power God has for us.

2 CORINTHIANS 13:3–4

If you're ever feeling weak, it makes sense. The truth is that you *are* weak as a human being. But God is not weak. Remember that with the Holy Spirit in you, you have the same power that raised Jesus from death to life working in you. That's incredible! Whatever God has planned for you to do, you can trust that you will not be weak at it. He will give you the gifts and strengths and tools you need to do it. And someday God's power in you will make you live forever in heaven too.

· ·

**Dear God, thank You that You are never weak.
You are my strength. You are my power. Amen.**

DON'T CHANGE YOUR MIND ON THIS

God is the One Who gives us power over sin through Jesus Christ our Lord. We give thanks to Him for this. So then, Christian brothers, because of all this, be strong. Do not allow anyone to change your mind. Always do your work well for the Lord.

1 CORINTHIANS 15:57–58

Do you feel like you can easily change your mind? Or are you someone who makes a decision or forms an opinion and then really sticks with it? You'll change your mind lots in life, some about big things and sometimes about little things—like realizing your favorite ice cream is not blue moon anymore, it's cookie dough now! But there's one thing to never, ever change your mind about, and that is trusting in Jesus Christ alone to save you from your sin and bring you to heaven one day.

• •

Dear God, I never want to change my mind about this: I believe You alone are the one true God, and Your Son, Jesus, is the only way to heaven because He died on the cross and rose again to save me from my sin. And I believe I have the power of the Holy Spirit in me to do the good works You created me to do here on earth until one day I'm in heaven forever with You. Amen.

HOPE COMES FROM GOD

*Our hope comes from God. May He fill you with joy
and peace because of your trust in Him. May your
hope grow stronger by the power of the Holy Spirit.*

ROMANS 15:13

Think about the things you hope for. You probably have a long list! What do you hope will happen at school tomorrow? What fun thing do you hope you'll do this weekend? What new birthday or Christmas present are you excited for? And what do you hope for the future, like the kind of family and job you want to have when you grow up? The reason we have any hope for good things at all is because God is the giver of hope. Every good and perfect gift comes from Him (James 1:17). And our ultimate, final hope is in heaven where there will be no more sickness, sadness, or pain, only perfect paradise. As you learn and grow each day, let your hope in God and His good gifts grow stronger and stronger by the power of the Holy Spirit in you.

• •

**Dear God, thank You for giving me hope. All good things come
from You, and I trust You have good plans for me here on
earth and a perfect forever waiting for me in heaven. Amen.**

MORE THAN CONQUERORS

Who can keep us away from the love of Christ? Can trouble or problems? Can suffering wrong from others or having no food? Can it be because of no clothes or because of danger or war? The Holy Writings say, "Because of belonging to Jesus, we are in danger of being killed all day long. We are thought of as sheep that are ready to be killed." But we have power over all these things through Jesus Who loves us so much.

ROMANS 8:35–37

Other versions of this scripture say that we are more than conquerors over any hard thing that tries to defeat us. Doesn't that make you feel strong and courageous? It should! There is absolutely nothing that can keep the love of God away from you.

• •

Dear God, when I am scared of anything at all, please remind me that I have power over it through Jesus! I am more than a conqueror because Your Holy Spirit is in me, and there is nothing that can stop Your love. Amen.

JESUS UNDERSTANDS

Jesus had to become like His brothers in every way. . . Because Jesus was tempted as we are and suffered as we do, He understands us and He is able to help us when we are tempted.
HEBREWS 2:17–18

Jesus became a human being, just like you are a human being. He grew up from a tiny baby, just like you are growing up. So He understands everything you go through, good times and bad. When you think about that, it can help you feel closer to Jesus. You can pray like this:

• •

Dear Jesus, I believe You understand what I'm going through right now. When You were in this world, You were sad and hurt and scared and angry and frustrated and tempted sometimes too, like I am. It helps so much to know that You know what all of this is like. But I don't handle all these things perfectly like You could, so will You comfort me and help me please? I trust that the Holy Spirit is in me to lead and guide me through every hard thing. I trust that You know and You care and You love me. Amen.

KEEP YOURSELF IN THE LOVE OF GOD

Dear friends, you must become strong in your most holy faith. Let the Holy Spirit lead you as you pray. Keep yourselves in the love of God. Wait for life that lasts forever through the loving-kindness of our Lord Jesus Christ.

JUDE 1:20–21

What are ways that you keep yourself in the love of God, like this scripture says? Do you spend time learning from God? Do you regularly read His Word? Do you talk to God through prayer and have quiet time to listen for answers? Do you go to a Bible-teaching church to worship and learn and serve there? Do you have other strong Christians in your life who help remind you and encourage you in God's truth and love? Do you fill your mind with songs of praise to Him? These are all awesome ways to keep yourself in the love of God! He never leaves you through His Holy Spirit, but sometimes it gets easy to ignore that He is there. So remember to keep yourself in His love every moment of every day.

• •

Dear God, I want to keep myself in Your love, staying in close relationship with You! Please help me never to forget or ignore You. Amen.

DON'T EVER SLIP AWAY

That is why we must listen all the more to the truths we have been told. If we do not, we may slip away from them.

HEBREWS 2:1

Have you ever made a giant Slip 'n Slide down a big hill? So fun! But there's a kind of slipping the Bible talks about that is no fun at all—the kind when someone forgets God's truths or just doesn't care about them anymore. We need to be careful we never let ourselves slip away from our love of God's Word and our willingness to learn from it. It truly is a lamp for our feet and a light for our path (Psalm 119:105). Without it, we are lost in this world.

• •

Dear God, I never want to slip away from loving and following Your truth found in Your Word. I always want to have great faith in You and love for You, the one true God and my Savior Jesus Christ. Amen.

GOD ABOVE ALL

It is God Who sits on the throne above the earth. The people living on the earth are like grasshoppers. He spreads out the heavens like a curtain. He spreads them out like a tent to live in. It is He Who brings rulers down to nothing. He makes the judges of the earth as nothing. . . . "To whom will you compare Me, that I should be like him?" says the Holy One. Lift up your eyes and see. Who has made these stars? It is the One Who leads them out by number. He calls them all by name. Because of the greatness of His strength, and because He is strong in power, not one of them is missing.
ISAIAH 40:22–23, 25–26

Look up into the night sky and remember that the one true God who cares for you made every one of those stars and calls them all by name. He sits on His throne above all the earth, and there is no one who can ever compare to Him. When the troubles in your life seem great, don't forget who is always greater—God your heavenly Father who loves you and lives in you through His Holy Spirit.

• •

Dear God, You are above all and greater than all, yet You see me, know me, love me, and live within me—wow! Help me be bold and strong and brave because I depend on You. Amen.

SCRIPTURE INDEX